MEDICAL REFORM:

BEING

AN EXAMINATION INTO THE NATURE OF THE PREVAILING SYSTEM OF MEDICINE;

AND

AN EXPOSITION OF SOME OF ITS CHIEF EVILS;

WITH

Allopathic Revelations.

A REMEDY FOR THE EVIL.

BY

SAMUEL COCKBURN, M. D.,

LICENTIATE OF THE ROYAL COLLEGE OF SURGEONS, EDINBURGH.

FIRST AMERICAN EDITION.

PHILADELPHIA:
RADEMACHER & SHEEK, No. 239 ARCH STREET.
NEW YORK:
WILLIAM RADDE, 300 BROADWAY.
1857.

MEDICAL REFORM:

BEING

AN EXAMINATION INTO THE NATURE OF THE PREVAILING SYSTEM OF MEDICINE;

AND

AN EXPOSITION OF SOME OF ITS CHIEF EVILS;

WITH

Allopathic Revelations.

A REMEDY FOR THE EVIL.

BY

SAMUEL COCKBURN, M. D.,

LICENTIATE OF THE ROYAL COLLEGE OF SURGEONS, EDINBURGH.

FIRST AMERICAN EDITION.

PHILADELPHIA:
RADEMACHER & SHEEK, No. 239 ARCH STREET.
NEW YORK:
WILLIAM RADDE, 300 BROADWAY.
1857.

PREFACE TO THE AMERICAN EDITION.

THE peculiar feature of our system, which distinguishes it from what is called the "orthodox" branch of the profession, is sustained by an ample array of erudite and convincing literature: enough, we think, to commend it to the notice and even serious consideration of all medical men who have a single desire for the development of truth and the advancement of science; so that they are left without excuse, and remain subject to judgment: —"*they who are blind le tthem be blind still!*"— But while this is the case, there is a decided lack of works which may appeal directly to the popular, or non-professional, mind of the community. The people, as a whole, will necessarily cling to an ancient faith, whether ethical, or philosophical, and for no better reason than that it *is ancient*, and *in the ascendant*, till cogent and convincing reasons force the more reflective and intelligent portion to dissent in such numbers as shall attract the vast masses who, unthinkingly, follow the leaders: and this we find not unfrequently the case, while they despise the feebleness and decrepitude, and distrust the ability to aid them in their need, of the miserable superstition which they cannot shake off. The Homœopathic school, though it has gained the confidence and approbation of many thousands, by the efficacy and success of its treatment, wherever its aid has been summoned,—too often only in the hour of extremity and despair,—has yet made few decided and commanding efforts to attract popular attention by such arguments as should be likely to gain consideration for its claims, before the hour of absolute hopelessness urges it as a last refuge.

It is therefore with much pleasure we welcome the republication of Dr. Cockburn's little work in this country, as it appears to us to be pre-eminently calculated to supply the vacuum hitherto overlooked by the members of our school. It is peculiarly adapted to the popular mind, being learned without pedantry, analytical without being abstruse, and scientific without technicalities. No intelligent person can give it an unprejudiced perusal and remain indifferent to the vast importance of the subject under consideration. We sincerely trust that every member of the profession in the country will place a copy of it in the hands of every family of intelligence within the circle of his professional and social acquaintance; and should they act upon our suggestion and follow our example—for we do as we teach—we will venture to predict that it will prove to be "bread cast upon the waters which they shall find after many days." But should many whom Homœopathy feeds and clothes refuse to aid in thus attempting to spread its principles more widely, we have the consolation still left that our art shall still flourish while they live upon it, and with renewed vigor when they are no more:—the vine, when stripped of its exuberant foliage and withered branches, glows with greener verdure and bends with the weight of more luxuriant clusters,—the sun has more room to lend its blessings to the crop, to dress it with beauty and endow it with strength.

CONTENTS.

CHAPTER I.

ALLOPATHY AND HOMŒOPATHY.

Allopathy a system of crude dogmas—Shuns investigation—Allopathic intolerance—Liberty of conscience—Necessity of learning before judging—Misrepresentation—Enmity to homœopathy—Popular faith in allopathy like that in paganism.. 11

CHAPTER II.

ALLOPATHY.

Origin of medicine—Medical theories—Allopathy a mixture of old theories—Allopathy made no real progress for 2000 years—Relation between allopathy and the collateral branches of medicine—Allopathic experience—Allopathic specifics—Allopathic palliation—Evils of—Allopathic sheet-anchors—Artificial drug—diseases — Allopathic medicines shorten the duration of life.. 20

CHAPTER III.

BLEEDING.

Its origin—A sheet-anchor—Inflammation—Notions about—What Inflammation is not—What it is—Bleeding in inflammation—Importance of the blood in the economy—Apoplexy —Notions about the disease—What is the cause of apoplexy —Effects of bleeding in apoplexy—Bleeding calculated to produce the disease—Bursting of a blood-vessel—Cause of—Effects of bleeding in such cases—Bleeding a man in the jaws of death—Diseases brought on by bleeding—Combe's opinion of bleeding—The "buffy coat" on inflammatory blood—Bleeding in inflammation of the lungs—Dr. Tod's opinion of—Injurious effects of.. 36

CHAPTER IV.

DOCTORS DIFFER.

Contradictory opinions about the nature and treatment of fever —Pericarditis—The effects of squills—Of opium—Doctors differ, case of—Contradictory opinions about consumption—About delirium tremens—Treatment of rheumatic fever, &c. —Causes of these contradictions—Remedy for.............. 61

CHAPTER V.

THE HOMŒOPATHIC LAW.

Prevailing ignorance on medical subjects—Prejudice in favour of allopathy—Origin of—Study of homœopathy—The curative relationship between a disease and the medicine which cures it—This relationship is the homœopathic law—Nature of disease—Pathogenetic effects of drugs—How to find out the curative relationship—Primary and secondary action of drugs—Doctrine of antipathy—Doctrine of similarity—Its relationship to facts—Proving of drugs on the healthy body—Importance of—Of no use to allopathy—Doctrine of antipathy impracticable—The homœopathic law the only safe and certain guide—All natural phenomena guided and regulated by law.. 70

CHAPTER VI.

OBJECTIONS AGAINST HOMŒOPATHY

Contradictory nature of—Homœopaths cure by imagination and by attending to diet and regimen—Homœopaths few in number—Homœopathy, if true, would have been sooner discovered—Some homœopathists have recanted—Homœopathy denies all the laws of physic and chemistry—The killing and curing powers of medicine—The small doses—These doses do not constitute homœopathy—Different degrees of susceptibility—Homœopathic remedies prepared to suit these—The dose must vary according to the effect to be produced—Dangerous and deadly effects of large doses—The power of small doses proved by experience—Erroneous information about small doses—Homœopathy opposed to common sense—And to the experience of the profession—Homœopathy proved a failure by Dr. Andral.. 86

CHAPTER VII.

EVIDENCE IN FAVOUR OF HOMŒOPATHY.

The practice of homœopathy not perfect—The law is—Allopathic scepticism in regard to evidence—Testimony of Hufeland—Rau—Hartmann—Evidence from general statistics—From a comparison of statistics in inflammation of the lungs—In pleuritis—In peritonitis—In yellow fever—Value of homœopathy in violent and dangerous diseases—Allopathic speculations about the nature and treatment of cholera—Destructive nature of allopathic treatment in that disease—Allopathic treatment in favour of camphor—Homœopathy and the Board of Health—Dr. Maclaughlin's testimony in favour of homœopathy—Allopathic and homœopathic statistics compared.. 110

CHAPTER VIII.

OPPOSITION AND PERSECUTION.

Case of Ambrose Paré—of Dr. Greenfield—Collegiate opposition to Homœopathy—And Denunciation of Homœopaths—Editorial Defamation and Slander—Dr. Combe and our opponents —Medical Directory and Homœopaths—Cause of Persecution. 138

CHAPTER IX.

ALLOPATHIC REVELATIONS.

Different Classes of Medical Men—Confessions of Dr. Forbes—of Bichat—Dr. Guy—Boerhaave—Gardner—Andrew Combe —Adam Smith—Dr. Routh—Paris—Professor Widekind—Hufeland—James Johnson—Franks—Reid—Krueger Hansen—Sir Astley Cooper—Keiser—Addison—Abernethy—Professor Gregory—Dr. Bailie—Dickson—Brown—Leeson—The Editor of the Lancet—The Medical Circular—Dublin Medical Journal—Medical Times.......... 152

CHAPTER X.

PROGRESS OF HOMŒOPATHY.

The necessity for Medical Reform—Progress of—Interest of the Public in this Reform—Allopaths must investigate Homœopathy, &c., &c. 174

PREFACE.

THE subject of Medical Reform is one that has agitated the Medical Profession for many years. All thinking men in the profession felt the need of reform, though none seemed to know the right remedy. At all events the profession could never agree among themselves as to what was necessary. Twenty-two years ago, an attempt was made to introduce a bill into Parliament to regulate the practice of medicine in this country; it failed. Repeated attempts have been made since then, but with no better results.

In the beginning of 1852, the Provincial Medical and Surgical Association for England proposed a Draft Bill, which was to represent the wants of the profession generally; but in place of that being the case, opposition bills were drawn out by the Scotch and Irish Universities, and by Sir John Forbes. The result was, that the Home Secretary was puzzled, not knowing what measure to support; and so dismissed them all.

During the present year a Medical Reform

Bill emanated from the Edinburgh University; but, as on former occasions, another bill was drawn out by the College of Surgeons in opposition to it. In May last, a deputation waited upon Sir George Grey. Sir George told them that, " on one occasion he remembered two deputations coming on one day, each representing, as they said, the general body of the profession, but they each espoused totally different principles—and, in fact, the bill to which he referred had been torn to pieces by the profession." No wonder that Lord Palmerston, on one occasion, intimated to a deputation that, the profession would require to learn to agree among themselves, before Parliament could do anything for them.

It appears to us that not one of all these bills could do any real good; even though they had passed into law. They would not have altered the practice of medicine one pin's point—that practice would just have continued to be what it has always been. And how could it be otherwise? The grand evil that lay at the root of all the others in practical medicine, was altogether overlooked and ignored by these bills. The great reform which was needed, was one which should make the practice of medicine *safer* in its application, and *more successful* in its results. No doubt there are many things connected with medicine that might be improved; but this is the first and most essential reform that is required in medicine. And our object in the following pages shall be to assist in bringing about such a reform; not by an appeal to Parliament, but to the judgment and good sense of the public.

In doing this it will be absolutely necessary to make an examination into the nature and extent of the evils and deficiencies which exist in the prevailing practice of medicine, so as to show that a great reform is actually required. And though in doing so, we may have occasion to use plain language, we distinctly and emphatically declare, that we have no personal bad feelings towards any in the profession, neither do we wish to give occasion to any one to entertain any personal animosity towards us. And though there may be many in the profession who have an hostile feeling towards the reform which we advocate, namely, homœopathy, still there are, we believe, some who, though differing from us in their views, are willing to give us a fair field, and meet us on common ground.

Homœopathy and allopathy must in their nature ever continue to be antagonistic to each other, and wide as the poles apart; still we believe that the present odious distinction which exists between homœopaths and allopaths is a great evil, and in the meantime to some extent injurious to the public. And for ourselves, we see no good reason why all duly-qualified medical men should not as such, co-operate harmoniously together; and agree to discuss the relative value of their systems, exclusively on their own merits. In this way the good and the true in medicine would be much sooner known and more generally acted upon; and what is false and injurious, sooner discovered and discarded.

We doubt not but that certain ulterior advantages will accrue to homœopathy by a continuation of the present sectarian distinctions, still we would gladly extend the right hand of fellowship to medical men of every creed and persuasion, and under one standard, though with different weapons, agree to do war against a common enemy.

SAMUEL COCKBURN, M. D.

Dundee, January, 1856.

CHAPTER I.

ALLOPATHY AND HOMŒOPATHY.

Allopathy a system of crude dogmas—Shuns investigation—Allopathic intolerance—Liberty of conscience—Necessity of learning before judging—Misrepresentation—Enmity to homœopathy—Popular faith in allopathy like that in paganism.

THE present state of the world is allowed by all to be one of great enlightenment, and such as demands a thorough revolution in all those fabulous and theoretical systems, which ignorance and self-interest have originated and kept alive. The supporters and advocates of such traditionary systems and practices assume the position and title of being wise, and condemn as silly and foolish everything that opposes their prejudices and inherited opinions. This has been, and still is the case, in regard to the supporters and advocates of the allopathic or orthodox system of medicine.

This system is a thing of the past, a product of the dark ages, and bears on its front the stamp of the times which gave it birth. It shuns the light and cannot stand investigation. Its advocates acting as judges, and condemning all who hold an opposite opinion, have assumed the prerogative of infallibility;

and by so doing, put a stop to all improvement. Like the priests in bygone ages, the medical hierarchs have done everything in their power to keep the world in ignorance of the true nature of their system, as a matter in which it had no concern; and in this they have but too well succeeded. All the other cognate sciences have been, and are still being, presented to the intelligent public in a form in harmony with the intellectual development of the age; elucidated and explained by more abundant and convincing modes of reasoning and induction; and supported by more self-evident and palpable facts which have been brought to light by the various discoveries in the arts and sciences. The allopathic system, on the contrary, stereotyped in notions the most obscure and dreamy; in speculations the most fanciful and unreasonable; in dogmas the most crude and absurd; is still kept concealed from public gaze in monkish seclusion, as a subject far beyond the comprehension of ordinary mortals, which none but those who have been initiated into the mysteries of the profession, and who have obtained the second sight, can at all pretend to understand. This has been the chief ground of condemnation of every false system of science and philosophy. Instead of courting investigation, by giving out its doctrines and principles in a clear and plain language, allopathy has all along shunned scrutiny: everything has been wrapped up in a dark and unmeaning phraseology. And as a proof and consequence of this, there exists at this present time, the most complete and universal ignorance in regard to the principles and doctrines of allopathic medicine among all classes of the community. No lack of knowledge in regard to the practice of the system; too many have learned this by a dear-bought experience. Those who can boast ignorance on that head are indeed a happy few.

It is a strange anomaly in history, that an individual, after having gone through a regular prescribed course of medical studies under prescribed teachers, and having been declared by a board of examinators to be thoroughly qualified to practice medicine, and having obtained a diploma to that effect, as a guarantee to the public, should yet, after that, be proscribed and branded as a quack and impostor, by the very same parties who gave the diploma; and that merely because the individual had added to his other medical attainments a knowledge of the principles and practice of a new system called homœopathy, and had so much honesty and candour as to declare his conviction of the superiority of that new system, over the principles and practice of the old or allopathic system; and yet it is true. This fact is in the highest degree humiliating to some of our university corporations and medical associations, and can be accounted for only on the ground that they knew very little about homœopathy; or, that actuated by a spirit of intolerance, they imagined that something very decided must be done *ex cathedra*, in case this new system should ultimately turn the world upside down, and bring their craft in danger.

Every medical man has a right to form an opinion of his own, but before passing judgment on any subject, it is his bounden duty to study the matter thoroughly and impartially. Without such a study, his opinion is a mere expression of his prejudice or ignorance. Allopathists are quite at liberty to differ from us, both in their creed and practice, so are we homœopathists at liberty to differ with them. We have no desire to force our views on any one, neither will we passively submit to the authoritative dictum of any party that differs from us. We allow to all the liberty we claim to ourselves, and wish to do to others as we wish them to do to us. Let the advocates of the old school come forward and expose homœopathy to the world. There ought surely to be some among such a large number who should be able to give a full exposure of the system, if it is either a delusion or quackery. One or two of no mean standing in the profession have attempted to do so, but the signal manner in which they have failed has deterred others from the task. Many who know nothing about homœopathy, properly speaking, are very decided in their talk against it, and would be very glad to expose it if they were able; not a few, who know something of the system, have their doubts and misgivings on the subject. They would not like to have their names handed down to posterity as opposing what might after all turn out to be a great truth; or as defending a system which is avowedly rotten and without foundation. They have their fears that homœopathy may, on some day not far distant, be so universally known and approved of throughout the world, as to become the ruling system and practice of medicine, and their names, alas! would be associated with dishonour.

Most of us have studied allopathy theoretically and practically for years. How long have any of our opponents studied homœopathy? Have any of them studied it closely for even *one* year, or even for six months? Have any of them had any practical experience of the system? If not, it is the height of presumption to pronounce against it. In coming to the study of homœopathy, it is not required to give up anything really useful, that has been learned either from experience or tuition; not at all. The more knowledge the better. But by all means come to a thorough understanding of the fundamental principle of the new system, become intimately acquainted with the facts and evidences on which it rests. If it is found to be untrue, there will be no difficulty in exposing its fallacy. And if found to be true, hold fast by it, and flinch not from advocating it. Do not condemn the system and abuse its advocates, while ignorant of the true character of both.

There are some medical men who seem to have peculiar notions about the responsibility which lies upon them when they speak about homœopathy. They spread reports about the system, and give explanations to others as to its nature and its power over disease, which we fear many of them *must* know, and what all of them *ought* to know, to be altogether untrue. There are even some, who are known to be men of high moral rectitude in other matters, who, nevertheless, are in the habit of making statements in regard to homœopathy, which are the very reverse of truth. Their ignorance of the system is not only no cloak to their blameworthiness in this matter, but is an aggravation of it. They ought to take the trouble to learn and know before they speak. Who of our opponents has done this? Who can lay his hand on his heart and say that he is free from blame in this matter? Who has overcome the power of self-interest? Who has resisted the power of custom and prejudice in searching after the truth of homœopathy? Let those answer who can. This is not a subject to be trifled with, or lightly laid aside, the health and lives of our fellow-men are at stake, and call aloud for serious, inquiring, and earnest investigation.

There are some men in the profession, the violence of whose opposition to homœopathy is more of the nature of enmity than anything else. It is they who have raised the cry, "Away with it, away with it. It is all humbug, quackery, charlatanery, imposture—its advocates are base impostors, and deserve nothing but extinction, root and branch." To such men we have little to say. They have had their analogues in all past ages, and in all time-serving systems. They have been, and still are, blots in society. But the day which shall try us, shall also try them.

As we are always ready to communicate to others what we have learned ourselves, so are we ever ready to receive instruction from those who have it to give; but kings and popes in medicine we do not acknowledge. That we must think and practice in this or that way merely because a certain party says so, under penalty of confiscation and excommunication, savours too much of the dark ages for us to listen to. We value the right of private judgment and freedom of conscience too highly, to become the slaves or tools of such despotism. Private judgment in the investigation, embracing, and defending of any new truth, is at once the right and privilege of every rational and intelligent being. And to that tribunal homœopathy makes its appeal. Every one has a vital interest in the relative merits of the two opposing systems of medicine; therefore be honest and sincere in investigating the subject. We pretend to no mysterious or secret knowledge, but are guided by plain, simple truth, which we desire others to share with ourselves. Did you ever hear of allopathic doctors inviting the public to investigate the truth of their system of practice? Did you ever hear of any one of them who ever made an attempt to prove the truth of their system? No, never. They dare not attempt it, because they know full well that it is impossible; and their evident object now is, as it has always been, to keep the public in ignorance by scholastic jargon, making them believe that they know far more than they really do.

The public at this moment are fearfully deluded in regard to allopathy, in imagining that they believe in its truth, when in reality they know nothing about it, and therefore cannot have any intelligent belief in it. Who knows anything about the foundation of the old system of medicine? Does any one? Let its advocates give a clear and intelligent statement and explanation of their principles and practices, apart from all mysticism, and thus give the public sufficient data to judge from. At present all such data are wanting, and the adherence to allopathy by the bulk of the public, has no better foundation than that given to paganism—it is purely of a traditionary character. In an age like this, such should not be the case. Every one should, in this matter, follow the example of the Bereans, and search in the book of facts, and diligently inquire into the volume of reason, to ascertain the truth for himself, no matter what the opinion of others may be. It was by following this course that Galileo discovered that the earth revolved round the sun, and not the sun round the earth. In the same way Columbus discovered America, and in this way Harvey discovered the circulation of the blood, and Jenner the use of vaccination. These and many other great discoverers dared to think for themselves; they were not content to follow the beaten path of those who had preceded them. They did not believe that whatever their fathers taught and believed must be true. They brought old-established theories to the test of experience—facts, and found them wanting. They proclaimed to the world their own discoveries, and invited men to examine them and test their truth. Each of these in his day suffered much persecution and ridicule. But the storms of ignorance and self-interest have died away, while the truths which they discovered still remain, and we enjoy the benefit of them. So will it be in regard to homœopathy.

CHAPTER II.

ALLOPATHY.

Origin of medicine—Medical theories—Allopathy a mixture of old theories—Allopathy made no real progress for 2000 years—Relation between allopathy and the collateral branches of medicine—Allopathic experience—Allopathic specifics—Allopathic palliation—Evils of—Allopathic sheet-anchors—Artificial drug-diseases—Allopathic medicines shorten the duration of life.

THE allopathic system of medicine, although upwards of 2000 years old, is very little, if at all, understood even among the best informed portion of the community, and with the great mass it is not understood at all. We are however not astonished at this, for besides the studied secrecy and mysticism in which that system has been shrouded, it is in itself essentially a confused, unscientific, and contradictory jumble of facts, theories and assertions, entirely destitute of any settled fundamental principle, by which the incongruous mass can be reduced to order and harmony. In the present chapter we shall endeavour, as briefly and clearly as the nature of the subject will admit of, to present the reader with some information on the subject, in order that he may be able to form an intelligent opinion as to its merits.

The practice of medicine in its origin, must have been in the highest degree, empirical. But man being endowed with a reflective mind, began to form vague speculations about the phenomena which he observed, and hence, at a very early period, medical hypotheses were invented. The first recorded theory is that of Hippocrates, who imagined that the cure of disease was to be effected by the evacuation from the system of certain diseased humours, called the *Humoral Theory*. Much of this system prevails at the present day, and forms the basis of the physicking doctors. Of these humours there were supposed to be a great variety, to each of which names were given. Galen reduced these to four cardinal humours, namely, blood, bile, pituita, and melancholia, and his theory flourished for a long time. After this, about the beginning of the sixteenth century, Paracelsus appeared and introduced a great many wild and fanciful notions; many of which were too grossly absurd to gain anything like universal credit among the profession. Still he succeeded in establishing a *chemical theory* decidedly opposed to that of his predecessors. The humoral and chemical theories prevailed till the middle of the seventeenth century, when the immortal Harvey discovered the circulation of the blood. All diseases were then referred to the energy or fulness of the heart, and upon this the *mechanical* and *hydraulic theories* were instituted. About the beginning of the eighteenth century, Dr. Stahl propounded a new theory called *Animism,* decidedly opposed to the mechanical theorists. According to this theory all the motions of the body were produced by the rational soul, and diseases were generally regarded as salutary efforts of this presiding principle to avert the destruction of the body. Among the followers of this system were some men of great eminence; they trusted almost entirely to the power of nature in the cure of disease, using only the most harmless and inert substances. They were the originators of what is now called the *expectant* system. The celebrated Dr. Sydenham held this notion of nature curing disease. Dr. Hoffman introduced a modification upon this theory; asserting that all diseases took their rise in the nervous system. Van Swieten, Haller, and others adopted and improved this system. The famous Dr. Boerhaave next introduced a very elaborate theory founded upon the humoral, and modified by the other prevailing notions. The well-known *Brown* next introduced his theory. General increase of action, or debility in each individual case, was the principle he adopted; and his practice in every case, was either a *stimulant* or a *sedative;* this system met with many supporters. Lastly, the system of *Broussais* appeared; he taught that almost all diseases were owing either to an *excess* or a *deficiency of irritability!* bleeding was his chief remedy.

With all these fanciful and conflicting theories, no decided improvement had ever taken place in the *practice* of medicine. There was no law—no fixed principle which could guide or assist the physician in selecting a remedy to cure disease. In this respect not a single step in advance had taken place from the time of Hippocrates. And it will require very little discrimination to see that, the practice of medicine prevailing in our day though neither entirely according to the one or the other of these theories, is yet nothing more nor less than a disorderly mixture of all of them. We have the humoral theorists with their physic and alteratives—we have followers of Paracelsus and the Alchemists with their powerful minerals and metals—we have the resuscitated doctrine of Animism in the modern expectant, or do-nothing system, with their bread pills and toast water—we have Brunonians with their artificial stimulants and sedatives—and we have the followers of Broussais with the leech and lancet. Strange that all these systems though more or less directly opposed to each other should have existence together; but stranger still that almost every so-called orthodox practitioner in Europe makes a public profession of his faith in each and all of these opposing systems by following them in his practice! This is the reason why the practice of medicine now a days is so complicated and contradictory, being composed of such a jumble of opposing theories.

Intelligent people are astonished to hear it stated that the practice of medicine in the hands of allopaths has made little or no progress for the last 2000 years. They have heard so much about the discoveries and improvements in and connected with medicine that they have always thought that the practice of medicine had undergone great improvements, and had mightily progressed—that in fact in our day it was in a highly perfected condition. In place of that, when we examine it and compare the practice of to-day with that of Hippocrates, we are inclined to think that the great father of medicine was not far behind any of his disciples. True, medical men have in the course of ages collected a vast mass of details and facts, but being linked together by no law or general principle, this heterogeneous mass is of little or no use to the profession; at most they can only add fresh material to the vast pile. The science of medicine proper is not to be confounded with the collateral branches. In surgery and the elementary branches of medical education, there have been many and great improvements; so much so, that at this time their progress is in harmonious keeping with the age we live in. But, while these branches—anatomy, physiology, chemistry, and pathological anatomy have made great and rapid advances, materia medica, (the knowledge of the medicinal properties of drugs,) and therapeutics, (the knowledge of the proper application of medicine in disease,) are wofully deficient; scarcely any progress at all has been made in these. As regards therapeutics, the progress has been so trifling, and its various parts so discordant, that no one can call it a science at all. And then the material composing the materia medica, is so meagre and so devoid of all method, as to render it, comparatively speaking, of little value in the treatment of disease.

Still we are told again that great advancement and progress have been made of late years in various departments of medical science. We remember one day having occasion to defend the claims of homœopathy against the attack of a clever allopath, and this was one of his objections (quite as appropriate by the way as most others that are generally advanced.) You homœopathists, said he, have made no great discoveries in medicines, while allopaths have made many; this shows that there are no great men among you. Now waiving for the present the fact that homœopathists have made more real and substantial discoveries in medicine during the past sixty years, than all the medical men that ever lived have done during the past two thousand, (but of these our aspiring allopath was profoundly ignorant,) what real practical good has resulted from these allopathic discoveries? One, like this gentleman, will instance Kiernan's discoveries in the structure of the liver, with which we homœopathists are quite familiar. But what good, we ask, is derived from this discovery in practice? Are allopaths more successful in their treatment of diseases of that organ now, than they were before such a discovery was made? This is the great question. Do they make more cures now than they formerly did? Facts say no. And in regard to discoveries in the anatomy and functions of the lungs and other organs, diseases of those parts are quite as fatal under allopathic treatment as they used to be. Such discoveries are not, and cannot possibly be of any service in the treatment of diseases. They teach us nothing about the properties of medicine, nor of their proper use in removing suffering, and that is what is wanted. All the collateral branches of medicine are highly useful in their own places, and the more we know of them the better; but a man may be a first-rate anatomist or chemist, and yet be practically ignorant of the treatment of disease: he might not be able to distinguish a case of measles from one of scarlatina, much less to treat the one or the other successfully.

But still we do not deny that there are some changes in practical medicine for good; they are becoming more and more apparent, and in one sense we rejoice to see them. First, there are a number of homœopathic remedies filched from the system of Hahnemann now somewhat extensively used in allopathic practice, and at times to good purpose, and second, there is much less medicine used and not a tithe of the bleeding practiced. These are great and important changes; but how have they arisen? Are they the development of allopathic progress? Assuredly not. For the two latter facts the world has in a great measure to thank homœopathy, and for the former, give the honour to whom it is due.

The allopathist examines his patient in order to form his *diagnosis*. The homœopathist examines his patient in order to find out every, even the most minute symptom of the complaint, so as to be able to select a remedy suitable for the entire disease. In the former case, the name alone is wanted, and the medicine is indicated as a matter of course, without any intelligent discrimination on the part of the physician. It is indigestion, it is bile, it is rheumatism, it is consumption, says the old-school doctor, and accordingly a medicine is given for the conventional name, and not for the exact and true disease under which the patient is labouring. On this account very little is gained by experience, even when the opportunities of gaining valuable information are most abundant. The following report affords a striking proof of this. The French Academy of Medicine have given a report of their experience in the treatment of typhoid fevers. The medical attendants, consisting of Andral, Louis, Bouilland, and others, physicked one hundred patients, without the slightest regard to symptoms, age, sex, or stage of the disease. They bled another hundred on the same plan: and with another hundred they did nothing. Now what could be learned from such indiscriminate, wholesale work as this; it is perfectly absurd. No one of any judgment could place any dependence at all on the results of experience like this.

The illustrious Zimmerman relates the experience of a physician of his own acquaintance, who used to arrange all his patients, between fifty and sixty in number, every morning into four divisions. To the first he prescribed bleeding; to the second, a purgative; to the third, a glyster; and to the fourth, a change of air! such is allopathic practice. The success of the painter lies in his catching the individual features and lineaments of his subject, and transferring these to his canvass. Even so the success and skill of the physician lie in his distinctly observing all the individual symptoms and peculiarities of each patient, and being able to select a remedy which corresponds to all these symptoms and peculiarities. This is the only scientific mode of practicing medicine. Names are useful enough in their own place, but we protest against their being made guides in practice.

Allopaths do occasionally make cures. Every medicine in their Materia Medica is valuable when properly applied, and they do from time to time stumble upon one which happens (in so far as their choice is concerned, by mere accident) to be homœopathic to the case, and thus unwittingly to themselves a homœopathic cure is effected. In their practice there are a number of remedies, the so-called specifics, which are frequently applied to good purpose. But, such remedies owe their existence in allopathic practice to mere accident. They are not the legitimate offspring of the system, they are isolated and estranged agents forced into an unnatural system, and in most instances applied to purposes for which they are not at all adapted. As a rule, these medicines are applied purely empirically without any knowledge of the ground of their adaptation. And cases are daily occurring in which the empirical doctor is baffled and confounded even while using those remedies which according to his orthodox notions ought to have been specifics for the disease. When we compare the little good that is done by the use of these remedies in the hands of allopaths, with the immense amount of evil that has been entailed upon suffering humanity by their abuse, it becomes a serious question as to whether it would not be better to give up the use of such remedies altogether; at all events, until some decided reformatory change should take place in the mode of employing them. Sir John Forbes says, "It would fare as well, or better, with patients, in the actual condition of the medical art, as more generally practiced, if all remedies, at least all active remedies, especially drugs, were abandoned."

The main stay of the old system in maintaining its sway over the public, is the practice of palliation. No one can form anything like a correct idea of the vast amount of mischief produced by this practice alone; but the subject is so important, and leads into such a large field, that we refrain from dwelling upon it here at any length. No part of the system is so successful as this in deceiving the sick and establishing the position of the medical adviser. The immediate apparent benefit generally derived from the use of these palliatives is such, as to lead the patient, who knows no better, to imagine that the doctor understands his complaint, and knows how to cure it. Alas! alas! that this should not be the case. The temporary benefit produced by such medicines is soon succeeded by a return of the old complaint, which again calls for a renewal of the old palliative. This goes on till the case becomes worse and worse, and also more complicated, so as entirely to destroy the comfort, and greatly to impair the usefulness of the individual; or, some new and more dangerous disease becomes developed, which suddenly destroys the patient; or, a truce for life is to come between the patient and his palliative, for the mere extension of a miserable existence. This system of palliation, of which at the very least three-fourths of the prevailing practice consists, fosters and harmonizes with the prevailing evils of the age. Present gratification is wanted; temporary indulgence, regardless of consequences. The world cries, Give us our stimulants, give us our purgatives, our stomachics, our tonics, our alteratives, our sleeping draughts, our soothing drops, our anti-spasmodics, our carminatives. Against one and all of this fraternity we protest; they are the enemies of health, the generators of disease, and the prolific sources of death!

The resources of the old school, though nominally very extensive, are practically, exceedingly limited. Take away their three great sheet-anchors—bleeding, purging, and giving of opium,—and what have they left? What could they do? Without these their occupation's gone. These form their chief stock in trade; all the other paraphernalia are the mere trumpery appendages of the three great idols. In fact one would be quite safe to say that, there is not a case of any serious disease in any part of the world under allopathic treatment, in which at least one, if not all of these destructive agents have not been employed.

In a very important sense these agents constitute allopathy; were they relinquished, the system is done to all intents and purposes. Bleeding, being by far the most important, and perhaps the most destructive of these agents, we shall address ourselves chiefly, if not exclusively, to the consideration of that subject. Before doing so, we shall say merely a word upon a subject that has been already adverted to, namely, the injurious effects of drugs on the constitution. The allopath knows nothing about the artificial diseases which the powerful drugs he is daily in the habit of using are capable of creating; and he never can know, until he takes the trouble to study homœopathy. He never dreams that in a great many instances, he is physicking the patient for the cure of a complaint which his own misapplied drugs have already produced; and yet cases of this kind are numerous. A vast number of patients are labouring under complicated drug diseases, produced entirely by long-continued allopathic treatment. Such persons are never in a state of sound health, and are seldom out of the hands of the doctor. Renewed doses of some new medicine frequently have a palliative effect and give temporary relief, and in this way the evil is made worse and worse, until the constitution of the patient is either entirely and permanently ruined, or some other more dangerous disease, induced by the former malady seizing upon a more vital organ, generally leading on to a fatal termination—so-called liver complaints, hypochondriasis, congestive headaches, rheumatic bone pains, &c., are frequently produced by allopathic drugging. Such patients have no chance whatever of getting better, until the true cause of their sufferings is understood, and proper remedies prescribed to destroy the baneful effects of the poison A physician, in Breslau, has a large collection of bones, in the cellular tissue of which, *numerous globules of pure mercury* are to be seen. In this country many instances of this kind are recorded.

A vast proportion of the most common and stubborn diseases are, to a great extent, manufactured by medical men. Thus an individual accidentally becomes confined in the bowels, (perhaps, by the way, a very salutary accident,) and he gets physic from the doctor. The primary action of the physic in opening the bowels is soon followed by renewed constipation more stubborn than before, and for this more physic must be taken. In this way the indications of nature are frustrated, and the constipation becomes confirmed—chronic; or, as the unfortunate patient is made to believe, constitutional. But the evil does not always stop here. The physic has an injurious effect on the rest of the system; upon the stomach, in producing a great variety of painful and uncomfortable symptoms, generally classed under the head of dyspepsia or indigestion. For these again, bark, or some other so-called *tonic*, must be given. The little relief afforded by these is of short duration; and besides a return of the former complaint, we frequently find so-called nervous and congestive headaches produced directly from the abuse of these fine tonics. Not only is this true in regard to strong drugs, such as mercury, arsenic, bark, &c., but it is equally true as regards the most simple and innocent medicines. Magnesia, for example, an article frequently recommended by doctors, and extensively used among children, produces most dangerous after-effects. On this point we shall quote the opinion of an influential allopathic journalist:—"That which is called the most innocent medicine may be the source of the utmost harm. Thus magnesia has been productive of fatal consequences. Masses unchanged have been found after death, closely collected together, or patches of the powder adhering with the utmost pertinacity to the intestines. Some very curious instances of this kind are upon record; and some of the cases have been, from the apparently suspicious circumstances, made subjects of investigation; for even deaths have been attributed to arsenic, when *post-mortem* examinations have shown that *magnesia* taken medicinally, not arsenic given as poison, was the destroying power." Think of this, you that are in the habit of using or giving magnesia.

A report of the Medical Society of London for 13th October, 1849, contains the following important remarks, bearing on this very point. Dr. Crisp said, "But as it regards the action of colchicum, I think the profession has yet the lesson to *learn* as to the *ultimate effect* of particular medicines on the *duration of life*, and I make this observation now in consequence of a remark made by Dr. Stokes, in Dublin; 'he had *never* heard of persons who had taken much colchicum living to a great age.'" Dr. Thompson also said, "I cannot refrain from referring to the observation of Dr. Crisp, as to the great importance of considering the *ulterior* effects of medicines." Take warning from this, you drug consumers—the ultimate effects of the use of particular allopathic medicines is to shorten the duration of life.

Dr. Wood, in a recent publication on Neuralgia, thus expresses himself on this very subject. "Some of the most melancholy cases of *Tic Doloureux* which I have witnessed, have been where opium has been given to mitigate the pain. Time after time the dose has increased, until, to the original morbid state, inducing the Neuralgia, has been *superadded the marasmus of slow opium poisoning.*" Dr. Wood is an opponent of homœopathy and no doubt speaks within the truth in regard to allopathic practice, he is one of its teaching professors, and would say nothing against it that was not too true, and yet from his testimony we are led to the conclusion that, the allopathic exhibition of opium in neuralgia, is such, as to induce the *marasmus of slow poisoning*—the gradual decay of slow and insidious poisoning. Dr. Wood says, he has seen cases of the kind. No doubt others have done the same. Who would take opium to mitigate pain, with this solemn fact staring them in the face; slow but sure poisoning?

CHAPTER III.

BLEEDING.

Its origin—A sheet-anchor—Inflammation—Notions about—What Inflammation is not—What it is—Bleeding in inflammation—Importance of the blood in the economy—Apoplexy—Notions about the disease—What is the cause of apoplexy—Effects of bleeding in apoplexy—Bleeding calculated to produce the disease—Bursting of a blood-vessel—Cause of—Effects of bleeding in such cases—Bleeding a man in the jaws of death—Diseases brought on by bleeding—Combe's opinion of bleeding—The "buffy coat" on inflammatory blood—Bleeding in inflammation of the lungs—Dr. Tod's opinion of—Injurious effects of.

The origin of the practice of bleeding is wrapped in mystery. Whether it was the result of theoretical reasoning, or the adventurous stroke of daring empiricism, is difficult to ascertain. One thing is certain, that it is not necessarily the product of any of the theoretical speculations of which the practice of medicine is composed. And yet, strange to say, it is practised by the propounders and advocates of every opposing theory. They all carry the lancet, as one of the many instruments of their art.

To say that bleeding may be dispensed with, in a great many cases in which it is at present had recourse to, no one will deny; but to affirm that it may and ought to be dispensed with in all cases, even those of acute inflammation and apoplexy not excepted, would appear to some as the height of madness. We once thought so too, and so did many others so long as the mere opinion of our teachers was our guide; but experience, and an impartial examination of facts, have convinced us of our error. We shall now endeavour as concisely as possible to present the subject in its true light, and leave the reader to digest the facts, and draw his own conclusions therefrom.

Requiring no skill in its performance, bleeding has ever been in practice one of the most convenient resources of the ignorant and unreflecting. In any sudden emergency, it does not much matter what it may be, one according to the orthodox faith and practice can scarcely ever be wrong to bleed. This, in fact, seems to be an axiom in the practice of a large majority of medical practitioners. When called to a case in which the pulse is full, rapid and bounding, all nature labouring under the influence of some hostile invader, bleed; remove a portion of the life and strength of the patient, in order to enable him the more successfully to struggle against and overcome the enemy: if one bleeding does not suffice to put an end to the strife, bleed again! or, if called to a case of accident, a blow or a fall, when the natural powers, stunned and enfeebled, are nearly at a stand still, bleed; bleed profusely, the blow has not completely taken away the life of the man, draw away some more life by bleeding, if the blood will run, so as to give him a better chance of rallying! Has a person been suddenly frightened, the heart throbbing strong and violently, bleed. If he has fallen down in a faint, the action of the heart all but stopped, bleed. Truly bleeding is a sheet anchor.

But an enquirer says, what would you do in a case of inflammation? you must bleed. People have got strange notions into their heads about this terrible thing they call inflammation. Thanks to their medical advisers for these. Before answering the question; can you tell us now what you understand by inflammation? this something which you and we dare say every one else thinks he knows well. For the most profoundly ignorant, and the learned, alike speak of it as though they knew all about it most intimately. Can you give us a definite answer as to what it is—

what it consists in? Try it before going any further. Do try, and you will find that all your notions on the subject are but vague and dreamy fancies, destitute of all definiteness and precision, and having no foundation in fact. Supposing a thousand individuals promiscuously without having any intercourse together, sat down to give their answer to this question, what a pretty set of answers we should have, to be sure! Before speaking of the treatment, we must supply an answer to the question, what is inflammation? what does it consist in? First then, as to what it does not consist in.

It does not consist in, neither does it depend upon, unnatural rapidity of the heart's action, consequently, nor of the rapidity of the circulation. For, the action of the heart, and the rapidity of the circulation can be, and often are vastly increased by mental emotions, and by exercise, while the individual is at the same time entirely free from all inflammatory action.

Second; it does not depend upon an increased quantity of blood in any particular part or organ. For, in the familiar act of blushing, the quantity of blood in the cheeks is frequently increased. Holding a part also before the fire for some time has the same effect. So also the reaction that takes place when a chilled part has been brought into a warmer atmosphere.

Third; it does not consist in the presence of too much blood in the body. For, during the inflammatory condition, there is no more blood in the body than there was previous to the inflammation. And it is absurd to think that there could possibly be too much blood during the inflammation, when, only an hour before, the person was in good health, and had not too much.

To bleed, then, under the idea that inflammation consists either in the one or the other of these conditions, would be the height of madness; but to the answer. You will scarcely believe when we tell you that, inflammation immediately depends upon an *enfeebled* state of the circulation, a diminution in its force and frequency, so much so, that in fact the blood-corpuscles actually begin to adhere to the sides of the capillary vessels, and ultimately stagnate there altogether. The minute arteries, owing to paralysis, or a state of exhaustion of their nerves, lose their natural healthy power of contraction, become relaxed and enlarged. Dr. Hooper accounts for this condition of inflammation in this way. "It is a general rule," he says, "that all stimuli applied to any part of the body call that part into action for a time, and that that action is dependent upon nervous influence; but the nervous influence suffers exhaustion proportioned to its intensity and duration, and that exhaustion produces in the part affected, a condition the very reverse of that which existed when the nervous power was in full force. The stimulant applied to a part determines the nervous influence to the small vessels of that part, and the function of those vessels—viz., their contractility, is for the time called into full play; exhaustion ensues, and then that same function is paralysed: in other words, the vessels lose their contractility, and yield to the blood that flows in them." The state of contractility, mark you, is not that of inflammation, it is the relaxed, exhausted, paralysed state that is inflammation. The Doctor thus further expresses himself. "There is then, no such thing as increased action of the arteries, in the sense in which that term is commonly used: that which used to be called *increased* action, is in fact *diminished* action."

This being the case then, that in inflammation there is diminished action, that is diminished contractility of the small vessels, and that the want of contractility is owing to a want of nervous power, how is it possible that blood-letting can in any way restore the blood-vessels to their former state of contraction? Just consider what is the cause of the relaxed condition of the blood-vessels. Is it the presence of their natural contents, the blood? surely not. Why then remove the blood? But an objector might say, the blood is in a bad state, that is the cause of it, and therefore we bleed. Well, we do not deny that the blood may be in a bad state. During inflammation all the secretions become vitiated, not only the blood, but those of the bowels, kidneys, and skin. But none of these are the cause of the inflammation, they are the effects. But besides, what good could possibly be effected upon the impure blood by bleeding? Could the removal of any quantity make what was left behind any better? Nothing but the exhibition of suitable remedies can possibly have any beneficial effect on the relaxed condition of the nerves on the one hand, and upon the vitiated state of the secretions on the other.

One of the chief causes of the great prevalence of bleeding among the old school doctors, is their erroneous views regarding the use and importance of the blood in the economy. It is scarcely possible to overestimate the importance of the blood. It is in a very significant sense the *life* of the being. And every ounce the doctor takes away, is nothing less than so much of the vivifying principle removed. As corroborative of this view, we shall give you the testimony of the celebrated German chemist, Liebig; at page 264 of his Organic Chemistry, he says, "The vivifying agency of the blood must ever continue to be the most important condition in the restoration of a disturbed equilibrium, which result is always dependent on the saving of time; and the blood must therefore be considered, and constantly kept in view, as the ultimate and most powerful cause of a lasting vital resistance, as well in the diseased as in the unaffected parts of the body." Any comment of ours on such testimony as this would be quite superfluous.

But the objector continues, what is to be done in cases of apoplexy, surely nothing but bleeding will do there? This has always been the clincher of the advocates of bleeding: and many a time have we had this question advanced by well-informed individuals, who could not get over the idea of bleeding being dispensed with in such cases. They spoke really as though they knew all about the nature of the disease, and as if they understood all about the how, and the why, bleeding was such an indispensable requisite in such cases. But on putting a few simple questions to such individuals, it soon becomes apparent that they are entirely ignorant of the whole subject, and have merely learned to re-echo the unfounded assertions of those interested in maintaining the orthodox practice.

Knowing that this is one of our opponent's strongest positions, we shall be at some pains to show, not only that the practice is erroneous, but that it is most pernicious and destructive. The most erroneous ideas exist in regard to the real cause and nature of apoplexy; and it is upon the assumption of the truth of these notions that bleeding is so extensively practised. The two principal ideas in connection with apoplexy are, first, that there is *pressure* on the brain, and second, that there is *too much blood* in the brain. How very learnedly and consequentially do these wiseacres speak about pressure on the brain, and too much blood in the head. These have been two most successful and convenient fabrications for imposing on the credulity of the public. There is pressure on the brain, therefore of course bleed to remove the pressure; there is too much blood in the head, therefore bleed to diminish the quantity. How very plausible does this sound. Can you believe it that this so-called pressure on the brain never occurs, that in fact there is no such thing, excepting perhaps in the doctor's own head, where there must often be pressure enough. Among other authorities we refer you to Dr. Hooper; at page 71 of his manual, he says, "Mere pressure then, does not affect the functions of the brain; when blood, serum, or lymph are found on the surface, or in the ventricles, or a tumour in the substance of the brain, or a larger quantity of blood than usual in some of its vessels, death is said to be occasioned by pressure. *This statement is incorrect; pressure there is none.*" Dr. Hooper, mind you, is no homœopathist, but a standard allopathic teacher.

The true cause and condition of apoplexy in place of being dependent on an excess of vital action, and a redundancy of arterial blood is, like inflammation, dependent on an entirely different and opposite condition, namely diminished action, that is, diminished contractility of the small vessels, and this diminished contractility owing to a deficiency of nervous power. We shall give you evidence from the well-known Dr. Latham, which bears on this very point. It is taken from the doctor's official report drawn up at the request of government, after an enquiry into the cause of the great mortality in the penitentiary. "An ox's head," he says, "weighing eight pounds, was made into soup for 100 people, which allows one ounce and a quarter of meat to each person. After they had been living on this food for some time, they lost their colour, flesh, and strength, and could not do as much work as formerly. The affections which came on during this faded, wasted, weakened state of body, were headache, vertigo, delirium convulsions, *apoplexy*." Was there too much blood, or an excess of vital energy in those persons' heads, think you? assuredly not. They were in that very condition in which a person is after being profusely bled; exactly so. And you can easily perceive that, as the faded and exhausted condition brought on by want was a cause of apoplexy, so bleeding, as it puts a person in the very same condition, also becomes a cause of apoplexy. In this exsanguined state, the arteries being deprived of their natural contents, become relaxed; the circulation through the brain becomes languid, and the capillaries pour out serum into the ventricles or on the surface, and the patient dies comatose. In such a case, a post mortem examination would reveal this effusion, in, or on, the brain; and this would at once be pointed out as the cause of the disease, whereas, in truth it was the consequence of the bleeding. Cause of death it may have been; but who was to blame for that?

We will now turn to facts and observations, in order to ascertain what evidence they give on this point. Sir Geo. Lefevre in referring to the treatment of apoplexy, and the increasing prevalence of paralysis, says. "It is not improbable that the universal system of blood-letting upon all such attacks, and even threatenings of them, has *converted remedial* into *incurable* diseases, paralysis has sometimes *immediately* followed the depletion *intended to prevent* apoplexy."

The well-known Dr. Clutterbuck in his article on apoplexy in the Cyclopædia of Medicine, says, "as mere matter of experience, there is reason to believe that blood-letting does much less good, and the omission of it less injury than is generally supposed." Although this is necessarily very guardedly expressed, you can easily see what effect experience and observation had produced on Dr. Clutterbuck's mind. Dr. Tod also thus expresses himself, in the medical circular for 12th April, 1854, " all cases of apoplexy are made worse by bleeding; we lessen the power of the system so to speak to throw off the disease." And then Dr. Copeman's cases. The Dr. had no fewer than 250 cases in his note book, though he gives us the specific treatment of only 150 of these. The following are the results: —

Number bled.........129	Cured.........51	Died.........78
Number not bled..... 26	Cured.........18	Died.......... 8

In his own words, he says "Of one hundred and fifty-five cases particularly specified, one hundred and twenty-nine were bled, and twenty-six were not; of the former number fifty-one recovered, and seventy-eight died; that is, nearly two-thirds. Of the latter, eighteen were cured, and only eight died; that is, somewhat less than one-third. In two cases, the temporal artery was opened, and both proved fatal; in fourteen cases, leeches were applied, ten died and four recovered; eighty-five patients were copiously bled with the lancet, fifty-seven died, and only twenty-eight recovered. "From these facts," continues the author, "it appears that bleeding, generally speaking, is so ineffectual a means of preventing a fatal termination of apoplexy, that it scarcely deserves the name of a remedy for the disease—that the treatment without loss of blood was attended with the most success, and the mortality of the disease increased, in proportion to the extent to which bleeding was carried—the more copious the loss of blood, the more fatal the disease."

The following case, too, which occurred lately, is also a striking proof of this view of the subject. We quote from a clinical lecture of Dr. Tod, physician to King's College Hospital. The case of a poor man, seventy years of age. "Though a well-marked case of apoplexy, he had none of the usual predisposing characteristics; none of what the Germans call 'habitus apoplecticus;' he had none of that full habit of body, with short neck, popularly known as belonging to apoplexy. On the contrary, he was *thin and half starved;*" as corroborative of that, the Dr. goes on to say that "his habits of living were described by his friends as miserly in the extreme, and we found he had two fits before, as he fell down in the street not long previously." In spite of the treatment the patient died, a post mortem examination took place, and among other facts observed, the doctor mentions the following: "The brain atrophied (wasted) the convolutions so to speak, shrunken, the subarachnoid space both large and containing a considerable quantity of blood," and further on, he continues, "in the left crus cerebelli a large blood clot." Now here is a well-marked case of apoplexy, with decided effusion of blood and fluid in the brain, evidently brought on by a weakened and impoverished state of the whole system. How could there possibly be too much blood in that man's body, or any rush of blood to the brain? the very idea of anything of the kind is absurd.

The following case, too is also in point. Toussaint L'Overture, who was incarcerated in the Chateau de Joux, by Napoleon the First, after being kept for a length of time on the lowest prison allowance, which in reality is just a slow process of starvation, was left for three whole days entirely destitute of food; when visited by his jailer, he was found dead in his cell. After examination, it was found, as certified by medical authority, that the immediate cause of his death was *apoplexy*.

The evidence given is most conclusive against the practice of bleeding in cases of apoplexy. No doubt there will always be some fatal cases resulting from this disease, under any mode of treatment, but all the chances of success are against bleeding. No one can possibly conceive of the dreadful havoc that the lancet has wrought in this disease alone, it is fearful. And then just think for a moment of the number of unfortunate creatures that are cruelly subjected to this dangerous treatment, even when there is no such thing as apoplexy about them. A person is suddenly seized with a fit, falls to the ground, the face is distorted, the brows knit, the eyes fixed and staring, or turned up under the lids showing only the whites; the arms are tossed about, and the hands clenched; the breathing is gasping, and foam issues from the mouth; the face is turgid and livid; the patient lies motionless and insensible; the doctor is sent for, and comes in all haste, in an instant the lancet is unsheathed, and the work of destruction then commences. The friends think that it is apoplexy, the doctor knows they expect him to draw blood, and the deed is done. Real and fatal apoplexy is either developed, or incurable paralysis is the consequence. Whereas, the mere application of cold water, and the exhibition of a suitable remedy might have saved the patient. Do not imagine that doctors cannot be mistaken in this disease, they are frequently mistaken, though the public know nothing of it. The following case of Dr. Graves, of Dublin, related by himself proves this; and when he made the mistake, you will not surely wonder at others having not a tithe of his knowledge and experience, falling into even greater blunders. "The gentleman," Dr. Graves goes on to say, "had slept well till four o'clock in the morning, when he was awakened by a general feeling of malaise, shortly after which he complained of chilliness, nausea and headache, after these symptoms had continued about an hour, his skin became extremely hot, the pain of the head intense, and drowsiness was complained of, which even ended in perfect coma, with deep snoring and insensibility; —in fact, he seemed to be labouring under a violent apoplectic fit. He seemed to derive much advantage from bleeding and other remedies, and to my surprise was perfectly well when I visited him in the evening.

The day but one after, at the very same hour, the very same symptoms returned, and were removed by the very same remedies." And was it cured now, think you? no, the symptoms again returned, and the Dr. goes on to say, that it was not till a *third* attack came on that he discovered his mistake, it being a case of fever and not of apoplexy at all. Had his patient died after the first or second attack, apoplexy would have got the blame, and not the bleeding, certainly not.

The following short statement from the Medical Circular, vol. 5, p. 107, also illustrates the same point. "Here to-day we find Rosina Schatta, age 37, said to die from apoplexy, but the medical man attached to the court has made a post mortem examination, and it turns out no apoplexy, but pneumonia."

The objector might ask again, what can be done in cases of hæmorrhage—bursting a blood-vessel? Could anything but bleeding do any good? Here again the most erroneous notions prevail. It is generally thought that, in such cases there is an excess of vital strength and a redundancy of blood, and, of course, bleeding must be had recourse to, in order to diminish these. Now in place of this being true, bursting of blood-vessels is invariably owing to debility.—It is a diseased condition, owing to a deficiency of vital energy and strength. Who are the subjects that are most liable to hæmorrhage? Is it the strong and healthy? no, but the delicate and the consumptive; these are undoubtedly the most frequent subjects of it. Almost every patient labouring under consumption, is at one time or other subject to hæmorrhage from the lungs. Strong, healthy lungs are not subject to hæmorrhage; and more than that, no part or organ of the body whatever can become the seat of hæmorrhage, unless in a diseased and consequently weakened state.

It is contrary to all experience to think that such a class of patients, and a disease of such a nature, could possibly be benefited by bleeding. Is it at all reasonable to think that, the opening of a new blood-vessel would be in any way likely to stop one that was already opened, and pouring out its contents in another part of the body? But hear what the celebrated Dr. Heberden says on this very point. "It seems probable," he says, "from all the experience I have had of such cases, that when the hæmorrhage proceeds from the breach of some large vein or artery, then the opening of a vein will not stop the afflux of blood, and it will stop without the help of the lancet, when it proceeds from a small one. In the former case, bleeding does no good; and in the latter, by an *unnecessary waste* of the patient's strength, it will do harm. But, if the opening of a vein be intended to stop a hæmorrhage by deprivation or revulsion, may it not be questioned whether this doctrine be so clearly established, as to remove all fear of hurting a person who has already lost too much blood, by a practice attended with the certain loss of more?" Dr. Heberden was long known as a first-class physician in London, and had an extensive practice; his judgment in this matter is therefore of much importance.

The following case from the *Lancet* is quite to the purpose, and may be taken as a fair specimen of all others of this class. The man had been quarrelling with his master about wages, when all at once he "turned deadly pale, and fell speechless and insensible for a time, breathing heavily until his neckerchief was loosed. In falling, his head struck the edge of a door, and received a deep wound three inches long from which blood flowed enough to soak through a thick mat on the floor." The man's wife immediately sent for a doctor, and got her husband conveyed to his own house, where he complained of pain in his head. The doctor came, and what did he do, think you?—bled him fearfully. One of the witnesses swore, that "she thought that about three and a fifth pints of blood were taken, besides what was spilt on the floor. The bleeding, she calculated, occupied twenty minutes." The consequence, as might be expected, was, that he never rallied from this bleeding, and died on the third day.

In the *Times* newspaper of the 22nd December, a case is given, which shows in a striking light the wretchedly absurd character of the routine practice of bleeding. "Mr. ——, surgeon, stated, that he was called upon to attend deceased, and found him at the point of death. He attempted to bleed him, but ineffectually, and in less than a minute from witness's arrival deceased expired. Witness not being able to give any opinion as to the cause of death from the symptoms that then exhibited themselves, he afterwards, with the assistance of Dr. Ridge, 37 Cavendish Square, made a *post mortem* examination, and found that a large cavity attached to the large vessel of the heart, containing blood, had burst, and that was the cause of death." Now here is a surgeon, called in to a serious case, about the nature of which he knows no more than the man in the moon, even according to his own confession, and yet, under the blind guidance of a false system, he has the hardihood to attempt to bleed the man, when in the jaws of death! This is no solitary case; it often happens that the lancet is employed when the medical attendant is entirely ignorant of the nature of the disease.

The diminution of pain generally brought about by bleeding, is a proof of the injury done to the nervous system; it produces partial paralysis of the nervous centres; it robs the system of part of its normal life and nutriment, and also deprives the heart of its normal and necessary amount of stimulus. Disease is in consequence of this, more able to overpower the vital force, and establish itself in the system, hence the many chronic complaints after bleeding. But it also gives rise to a great many serious complaints, among others, Darwin says, "a paroxysm of gout is liable to recur on bleeding."—John Hunter mentions "lock-jaw and dropsy."—Travers has observed "blindness and palsy."—Marshall Hall, "mania."—Blundell, "dysentery."—Broussais, "fever and convulsions."—Majendie, "pneumonia, and an entire train of what people are pleased to call inflammatory phenomena; and mark," he says, "the extraordinary fact, that this inflammation will have been produced by the very same agent which is daily used to combat it." You see that there is a superabundance of testimony to the evil effects of blood-letting; but, as the subject is one of paramount importance, we shall still further adduce evidence against the practice.

Our first authority is the talented and highly esteemed Dr. Combe. Speaking of the old school practice, in a letter which appeared in the British and Foreign Medical Review, he says, "Relying upon the testimony of an incomplete fact, the moment the practitioner ascertains the existence of inflammation, he pulls out his lancet and bleeds his patient copiously. The oppressed vessels being then partially emptied, much relief is experienced, and both patient and physician are pleased with the hope that the disease will be 'cut short.' In a few hours, however, the vessels have contracted, and they and the heart have adapted themselves to their diminished contents, and nature thereupon resumes the attempt to carry the disease through its proper stages. The pain returns, the pulse rises, and the oppression augments. Bleeding is again resorted to with immediate relief, and the same phenomena recur." He then goes on to add, that with a good constitution and good management the person may survive, but if the constitution is not robust, he "falls into chronic disease," with an impaired constitution, "his strength permanently shaken," and "ultimately dies." Such is Dr. Combe's opinion of bleeding in inflammatory diseases.

The facts connected with the case of Lord Byron are also full of interest on this point. During his last illness, it was with the most intense reluctance that Byron would consent to allow himself to be bled, when he at last did consent, Mr. Millengen writes "We seized the moment, and drew about twenty ounces. On coagulation, the blood presented a strong buffy coat; yet the relief obtained did not correspond to the hopes we had formed; and during the night the fever became stronger than it had been hitherto, the restlessness and agitation increased, and the patient spoke several times in an incoherent manner. On the following morning, the 17th April, the bleeding was repeated twice (!!) and it was thought right also to apply blisters to the soles of his feet."—the rest of the tragedy is soon told, he died the next day. Mr. Millengen and Dr. Bruno, were Byron's medical advisers; besides being misled by the false theory about inflammation, the presence of the so-called buffy coat, misled them still further. This buffy coat they (and so do many still) looked upon as an infallible sign of inflammation, and an indication for a further bleeding. Now the truth is that, the buffy coat is no sign of inflammation at all; for we find it distinctly present in certain states of the system when there is no inflammation whatever. Dr. Hooper says "a genuine and well-marked buffy coat, with retracted and puckered edges, may be found in the blood, although there be no inflammatory disease present." The mere presence of the buffy coat, therefore, is by no means an indication of the existence of inflammatory action.

Inflammation of the lungs being a disease of frequent occurrence, and one in which bleeding is generally had recourse to, we will now examine the results of such treatment, in order to find out whether it is beneficial or injurious. Dr. Tod, late professor of medicine in King's College, thus expresses himself on this subject: "The plan of treatment which has been recommended by some of our highest authorities, I need not tell you, is that of bleeding and tartar emetic; you bleed early from the arm, and, if necessary, you bleed a second and a third time, and if under this treatment, resolution (cure) does not rapidly take place, you bleed locally by leeches and by cupping, and likewise give tartar emetic more or less freely; to all which, counter-irritation (by blisters) may be superadded in the more advanced stages. I have had ample experience," he says "of this treatment, and I must confess, that expérience has so little satisfied me with it, that I have for some years ceased to adopt it; for under the treatment I have seen too many die; and where recovery has taken place, in too many instances has it been with a tedious, lengthened convalescence."

Speranza, in his annals of medicine has published some remarkable observations, which show that, the number of deaths in cases of inflammation of the lungs, is in direct proportion to the number of bleedings. In one hundred cases in which bleeding was had recourse to more than nine times, sixty-eight died; and in one hundred cases in which bleeding was had recourse to from three to nine times, twenty-two died; and in one hundred cases in which only three bleedings were resorted to, nineteen died; and in one hundred cases in which there was no bleeding, only fourteen died. These cases stand thus:—

100 cases, above 9 times bled.............68 deaths.
100 cases, from 3 to 9 times bled.........22 "
100 cases, only 3 times bled................19 "
100 cases, not bled at all..................14 "

Average mortality of the three hundred cases that were bled, 33·9 per cent.; average mortality caused directly by the bleeding, 19 per cent! In the first one hundred cases, the prodigious number of fifty-four! were sacrificed by bleeding, how dreadful! fifty-four human beings put to death by the lancet. Well might Sir Charles Bell declare towards the end of his career, that the lancet was the death of thousands.

Dr. Dietl, of Vienna, no homœopathist, mind, has also made very important experiments relative to the influence of bleeding and tartar emetic in inflammation of the lungs. Eighty-five cases were bled, and of these, seventeen died. One hundred and six were treated with tartar emetic, and of these, twenty-two died. One hundred and eighty-nine cases were left to unaided nature, and of these only fourteen died.

Thus, 85 cases, bled	17 died	20·4	per cent.
" 106 cases, tartar emetic	22 "	20·7	"
" 189 cases, left to nature	14 "	7·4	"

Dr. Dietl further adds, "we cannot forbear this expression of our belief, that venesection favours the spreading of hepatization, and favours it all the surer the oftener it is repeated, and the poorer the patient is in blood,—so that many pneumonias, both intense and extensive are pushed to their height by venesection—progressed and throve, so to speak, under the lancet." And still further on he adds, "we have not unfrequently remarked, that a single venesection, apparently well indicated, had, as consequences, striking sinking of strength, profuse sweat, miliaria, vibrating pulse and a rapidly fatal termination;" and also "that venesection has its certain and not unimportant share in the great mortality of pneumonia."

The mortality in Dietl's cases are not nearly so great as those of Speranza, and for this simple reason, that he did not push the bleeding to the same extent. We may look upon Dietl's success as being equal to that of the best practitioner's of the same class, namely, twenty per cent. deaths. Taking this view, we have thirteen out of every hundred destroyed by this treatment; what an enormous number must be killed in the course of fifty years by allopathic interference. No wonder that Dr. Reid in his Essays, was constrained to say, "that less slaughter is effected by the lance than by the lancet—that minute instrument of mighty mischief." Further evidence of this kind could be given, but we consider that enough has already been adduced to convince any unprejudiced mind, that the allopathic practice of bleeding, is not only unnecessary, but that it is highly injurious; and in a great many cases deadly in its effects.

CHAPTER IV.

DOCTORS DIFFER.

Contradictory opinions about the nature and treatment of fever —Paricarditis—The effects of squills—Of opium—Doctors differ, case of—Contradictory opinions about consumption—About delirium tremens—Treatment of rheumatic fever, &c. —Causes of these contradictions—Remedy for.

THE fact that medical men do differ from each other is one proverbially notorious, though the true nature and extent of that difference is not generally known. Some imagine that it is a mere difference in opinion and theory, and not one that pervades and characterises the whole of their practice. We shall therefore adduce a few of the differences that prevail among our orthodox allopaths.

"Fever," says one, "is nothing but debility;" "fever is nothing but inflammation," says another; "fever is a mobid condition of the stomach and bowels," says a third. One gives wine, the other draws blood, and the third gives purgatives, while another party of the same school, disgusted with such contradictory ideas, and such empirical practice, prefers leaving nature to herself, believing with a well-known American physician, that "those who are left to God's providence and cold water have the best chance of success." Another says that "all fevers arise from inflammation or irritation of the mucous membrane of the intestinal canal," which is proved from the post-mortem examination of patients who die of fever; and the true practice is to keep the patient on low diet, with cooling drinks and gum water. Another says that "fevers are caused by inflammation of the brain," and therefore the patient's head must be shaved, ice applied, and a dozen of leeches to the temples, besides he must be bled freely from the arm, and get a brisk purge.

Dr. McLeod, a Fellow of the Edinburgh College, relates what came under his own observation in the Edinburgh Infirmary, in regard to the treatment of fever. "Three young persons, each about the same age, ill of typhus fever, were admitted into the infirmary on the same day. The disease was in the same stage and of equal severity in each case, but they were each under the charge of different physicians. One would naturally expect that in the same institution, and at the same period of time, the three similar cases would have met with similar treatment. But no, the one patient was bled with lancet and leech, the other was physicked with drastric purgatives, and the third got whisky, wine and opium." So much for uniformity in practice in the nineteenth century, and for the result of being guided by so-called "general principles," (pure fancies.)

In the University a learned professor was lecturing on the subject of *pericarditis*—inflammation of the investing membrane of the heart. He spoke of the general practice of giving mercury in large doses, so as to bring the system under its action as speedily as possible; combining the mercury with small doses of opium. "This practice," he says "I believe to be erroneous; for I have observed the progress of the disease unchecked, even during profuse salivation. The most efficient remedy—in fact our sheet anchor in this disease, is tartar emetic. You will have noticed the large doses I have given of this remedy, and yet the patient seems not to suffer from it." Four nights after, another professor in the same hall happened to lecture on the same subject, and expressed himself to this effect, "It is a remarkable thing that, there should be any difference in regard to the treatment to be pursued in such a case as this. I believe it is the Italian and French schools which advocates so very strongly the employment of tarter emetic; but I would strongly urge you to put no confidence in this remedy; for, if you do so, you will lean on a broken reed; our sheet anchor in this disease is mercury." These are specimens of the instruction! that young men receive at our Universities, as well as specimens of the practice they are to follow! Surely when we find such contradictions among teachers and professors, we need not wonder to find still more glaring contradictions among ordinary practitioners, who can have no pretensions to the deep lore of teaching professors.

Dr. Neligan, a standard authority, says, in regard to squills, that, in consequence of its stimulating effects, it is inadmissible where there is any tendency to inflammation. Dr. Christison, on the other hand, a no less accredited authority, says, that "it never stimulates the circulation, neither is there any sound reason for avoiding it in acute affections of the chest, on account of its supposed stimulant operation." We leave the reader to judge which of the two gentlemen is right. The whole domain of medical science abounds with similar contradictions, which if only half known would astound men by their enormity, and startle them from their fancied faith in the allopathic practice of medicine.

Dr. Pereira, in his Elements of Materia Medica, says, Dr. Murray and Dr. Thomson believe that opium is a stimulant; Dr. Cullen regards it as a sedative; Dr. Mayer thinks it is both stimulant and sedative; Orfila thinks it is neither the one nor the other.

Dr. Bordeu, in his researches upon mucous tissues, tells us that he made the fourth doctor called in to consult about a patient labouring under fever, pain in the side, and bloody expectoration. "It is easy to understand," he says "that I had no advice to offer;

one of the gentlemen insisted on a third bleeding, (it was the third day of the disease,) the second upon a compound purge and emetic, and the third upon a blister to the thighs. The debate raged high; neither would yield an atom, and for myself, I could have sworn that each one was right in his turn." Patients and relations know nothing about these so-called medical consultations; the policy of the physician requires the external semblance of unity and harmony before the public, while within all is contradiction and confusion.

Stahl, attributes the frequency of consumption to the introduction of Peruvian bark; Morton, considers the bark as an effectual cure for that complaint. Reid, ascribes the frequency of the disease to the use of mercury; Brillionet asserts, that it is curable by this metal only. Rush says, that consumption is an inflammatory disease, and should be treated by bleeding, purging, cooling medicine, and starvation; Salvadori says, it is a disease of debility, and should be treated by tonics, stimulating medicines, and a generous diet. Galen, recommends vinegar as the best prevention of consumption; Desault and others, assert that consumption is often brought on by a common practice with young people of taking vinegar to prevent obesity. Dr. Beddoes, recommends foxglove as a specific in consumption; Dr. Parr, found foxglove more injurious in his practice than beneficial. Dr. Young, an author on this subject, says, that "the want of proper nourishment is the most frequent cause of consumption." Dr. Lamb, a no less trust-worthy observer, asserts that "an excessive use of animal food is among the most prominent and prevalent procuring causes of the disease." Doubtless there are many more contradictions equally glaring as these, even in regard to this single disease. Consumption is at all times a dangerous malady, and difficult to treat successfully; but really, with such contradictory ideas about the nature and treatment of the disease by allopaths, it is not to be wondered at that they are entirely baffled with it. Of late years this disease has been greatly on the increase. From the Registrar General's Report, it appears that, sixty thousand die every year of this complaint in the British Isles; besides the great numbers that leave the country and die abroad. In the town of Glasgow alone, with a population under 400,000, 2,133 die of consumption every year!

Armstrong thinks that *delirium tremens,* is a venous congestion of the brain and liver, consequent upon the activity of the heart and arteries increased by irritation. Playfair, thinks it arises from a morbid state of the liver and intestinal secretions. Golden says, it has its seat in the solar and cœliac plexuses, and looks upon the affection of the brain as being merely sympathetic. Clutterbuck, thinks it is the consequence of inflammatory action in the *arachnoid* and *pia mater*. Hufeland, believes it to be only a passive nervous delirium. Stokes again says, there are two kinds of it, one consisting in diminished irritability, the other in increased excitement. Every one has his own peculiar theory, and thereon he builds his practice. It is not the sufferings of the patient that indicates the kind of treatment, but the doctor's theory.

In rheumatic fevers, one will give colchicum; another mercury; another trusts only to purgatives; another has faith only in sudorifics; another, again, has no faith in anything but opium; another prefers quinine; another thinks that nothing but bleeding will do any good; another will give alkalies; another holds by lemon juice; and many again believe that all kinds of treatment are alike useless. Of this number was the late Dr. Warren, who, when asked his opinion about the best way to treat rheumatic fever, laconically replied, "*six weeks.*"

Even in the investigation of diseases, we find the greatest difference and contradictions prevailing among allopaths. The celebrated Sydenham, in speaking of the examination of dead bodies, in order to discover the nature of diseases, says, "It must be confessed there is some specific property which no contemplation reduced from the speculations of the (dead) human body can ever discover;—whereby that man should not so place the main of the business upon the dissection of carcasses, as if thereby the medical art might be rather promoted, than by the diligent observations of the *natural phenomena*, and such things as *do good* and *hurt.*" On the other hand, Dr. Bailie says, "The dead body is that great basis on which we are to build the knowledge that is to guide us in distributing life and health to our fellow creatures."

Dr. Billing, in his Principles of Medicine, thus expresses himself: — "The so-called systems of Cullen, Brown, Braussais, Rasori, &c., seemed mere individual opinions, totally differing from each other: and which was I to follow? Each of their originators seemed confident; while their followers almost came to blows, arguing as much for victory as the love of truth."

It would be endless to trace out all the differences that exist among old-school practitioners, both in theory and practice; the history of medicine is full of instances of the kind. One man's opinion or theory is just as good as another's; and as the practice of each is founded on the special theory, so the practice of the one is just as good as that of the other; they are all different; can they all be right? The cause of all these differences is, that, in allopathy there is no settled, no fixed principle by which the practitioner can be guided in his practice—there is no certain nor definite data, all is conjecture and theory. Even the use and virtues of certain remedies frequently employed, are of a very doubtful and fanciful origin. Tom told Dick, who handed it over to Harry, that such and such a medicine was good for the jaundice. Jenkins informed Robertson, who handed it over to Brown, that he heard it from the celebrated Stiggins, that such a medicine was a cure for the rheumatism. Each one must just be led by the theories or practice of some other one whom he looks up to. Every one has his own favourite or favourites, and that or these he follows, right or wrong. Every age has had its oracular men, its Stiggins, and Jenkins, and so has the present. Dr. L. after physicking away at his patient for many years to no good purpose, sets off in his extremity to Professor S., as if he were the veritable Delphian Oracle, and from him gets some novel prescription. Or may be, he goes to Professor C., another of these oracles, (the teaching Professors already referred to), and laying aside any judgment of his own, allows himself to be guided entirely by the prescription of his master. One oracle says one thing; another oracle says another and a very different thing, and so the game goes on.

The remedy we propose for all this, is one both simple and efficacious:—One that introduces order and harmony, in place of confusion and disorder :—

that gives precision and confidence, in place of doubt and uncertainty; that delivers the physician, from the bondage and servility of being obliged to make the mere dictum and fancy of others his only guide in practice; and supplies him with data, by which he can, if he exert himself, choose with certainty, the curative remedy in any given case. This remedy is Homœopathy, the nature of which we will explain in the following chapters.

CHAPTER V.

THE HOMŒOPATHIC LAW.

Prevailing ignorance on medical subjects—Prejudice in favour of allopathy—Origin of—Study of homœopathy—The curative relationship between a disease and the medicine which cures it—This relationship is the homœopathic law—Nature of disease—Pathogenetic effects of drugs—How to find out the curative relationship—Primary and secondary action of drugs—Doctrine of antipathy—Doctrine of similarity—Its relationship to facts—Proving of drugs on the healthy body—Importance of—Of no use to allopathy—Doctrine of antipathy impracticable—The homœopathic law the only safe and certain guide—All natural phenomena guided and regulated by law.

THE wide-spread and almost total ignorance that prevails among the public in regard to the properties of medicine and the nature of disease, is one of the most important causes of the entire want of progress in the healing art; we have no wish that every man should be his own doctor, certainly not; but still we hold that, every man ought if possible, to put himself in possession of such an amount of knowledge of these subjects, as shall enable him intelligently to choose his medical attendant, and not be left entirely to the tender mercies of chance and empiricism. There are thousands, who will discuss for days together, almost any of the most difficult points in theology, who at the same time know nothing at all about the constitution of their own bodies, or the diseases to which they are exposed, or of the means of curing themselves. Surely, if men of ordinary intelligence are capable of understanding subjects so exalted, and necessarily so difficult, they ought to be equally capable of understanding the constitution of their own bodies, the nature and principles of medical treatment. Once get the public enlightened on this subject, and their pressure will to a certainty compel the abettors of the orthodox faith, to bestir themselves and keep in advance, otherwise they will be pushed aside.

People have always had the notion that the doctor is acquainted with certain specific remedies for every disease; and that the disease only requires to be known, for the doctor to go at once for the exact specific. Pity it is, that this is not true. No wonder the public are prejudiced in favour of the orthodox faith of their fathers. No sooner is a child born, than it must have a cleansing with castor oil; no sooner does the little thing begin to fret, perhaps in consequence of some indisposition or indiscretion of the mother, than it must be drugged with Dalby's Carminative or Soothing Drops. For every little ailment that shows itself during teething, it must have its rhubarb, calomel, or jalap, or perhaps all three combined. No sooner does he reach boyhood, than his blood must be cooled and purified, by regular doses of calomel, salts, senna, &c. In youth and manhood, he is gradually, and it may be unconsciously, initiated into the faith that, bleeding, blistering, purging, vomiting, and sweating, are the only true and proper means for curing disease. When attacked with sickness, he submits himself to this orthodox system, merely because he has been taught that it is orthodox. But he never thinks of making an enquiry as to whether this system is really true in itself, and therefore likely to be beneficial in its application; or whether it is fallacious in its whole structure, and, therefore, necessarily injurious in its consequences. And what in times past has been true of the public in this respect, is not less so of the profession. They will not be prevailed upon to study the claims of homœopathy; they have decided against it in ignorance, and there they take their stand.

In coming to the investigation of the truth of homœopathy, there is one fact that must be clearly understood and kept in view, namely, that medicines really have the power of curing disease, and that, betwixt the disease on the one hand, and the medicine that cures it on the other, there must be some relationship, on the ground of which the medicine does cure the disease. It is this relationship which in any particular case, forms the groundwork of *adaptation* between the medicine and the disease. In practice, it is of paramount importance, nay it is indispensable that we should know this adaptation. It will not do, in any case, to go on trying this medicine, and that medicine, and then something else, and leave the adaptation to mere chance; or merely hope that the one or the other medicine may be adapted for the cure of the disease. This is opposed to all scientific practice, and fatal in its consequences to the sick. As already stated, practical medicine must have been in its origin, purely empirical and experimental, but it will never do for us to go back to the rudeness and ignorance of the uncivilized savage. Though we shall by and by show you, that we have the advocates and followers of such practice among us yet, differing only in the mysticism and technical lore they have succeeded in throwing around their practice.

The nature of the disease, including its structural and functional phenomena; the properties of the medicine, including the various effects that it is capable of producing upon the structure and functions of the body; and lastly, the curative relationship that subsists between medicine and disease, must all be known, before medicine can be safely and successfully practiced. Homœopathy as a system includes all these; but, as the two former naturally develop themselves from the curative relationship, our object at present will be to establish the latter—generally called the Homœopathic Law.

All disease consists of, either functional derangement, or structural change; and these it is the duty of the physician most carefully and minutely to investigate. The functional derangement and structural change, are termed the *symptoms*, and when all taken together, they constitute the entire disease.

Every medicinal substance, when taken by a person in health, alters and disturbs in some way the natural healthy functions; and also, when continued for any length of time in considerably large doses, produces structural change. This alteration of function, and change of structure produced by the medicine, is called its *pathogenetic effects*. The terms medicinal property, and artificial, or drug disease, mean the very same as pathogenetic effects. Apart from these pathogenetic effects, or the disease-producing power, no medicinal substance possesses any virtue in the cure of disease; and it is only when this disease-producing power is properly applied, that it becomes a health-producing power, or curative agent. It is obvious that, to apply medicine properly, we must first be acquainted with its disease-producing property. It is true that, one may chance at a time to make use of a medicine, the properties of which he is entirely ignorant of, and yet do good with it; but such a mode of practice is pure haphazard work, and entirely unscientific.

On making a comparison between all the symptoms functional and structural, of any natural* disease on the one hand; with all the symptoms structural and functional of an artificial or drug disease on the other, we find one of the following relationships existing—1st, Either a similarity between these symptoms, or 2nd, a contrariety or opposition, or 3rd, a dissimilarity, but not contrariety. There cannot possibly be another, and it must be on one of these three, that the true healing art is based. In any given case, a medicine that effects a cure, must do so, on the ground of one of these three relationships; and our present object will be to find out which of these it can possibly be.

Every medicinal substance, as has been already stated, when taken into the system, produces a distinct and direct train of symptoms peculiar to itself,

* The term natural disease, means any disease that occurs in the course of nature, such as scarlet fever, measles, cholera, &c.

which are called the pathogenetic effects of the medicine; but, we find that, after a short time, a reaction of the system takes place against the drug, whereby the primary effects of the drug are displaced, and a condition the very opposite of the first effects of the medicine is established. In other words a secondary action takes place, the very opposite of the primary action. (See the reason of this by Dr. Hooper, at page 40, line 22.) Suppose, then, that a medicine, the symptoms of which are contrary to those of the disease, be given to cure that disease; it follows, as a rule, that, if the dose of the medicine be of sufficient strength, the symptoms of the original disease are for the time being stopped; but that the disease itself is not cured, is evident from the fact that, so soon as the primary effects of the remedy are over, the secondary, opposite effects make their appearance along with a renewal of the disease, and that generally, in an aggravated form. This is true in regard to every kind of medicine when given on this principle; and is familiar to every one in the case of purgatives being succeeded by constipation, astringents by looseness, stimulants by depression, narcotics by restlessness, &c. They all generally answer the purpose for which they are taken, and that is, for the time being to palliate, though in the long run, they invariably aggravate the complaint, and exhaust the vital powers. It is evident, therefore, that this cannot be the curative relationship, and that therefore a system of medicine founded on this relationship, must be destitute of all curative power; this the experience of the past 2000 years has proved to be the case.

Then as regards the other relationship, namely, that of dissimilarity only, it will be at once manifest that, if the symptoms of the drug are neither similar nor opposite to those of the disease, the action of the drug must affect entirely different functions, and in many cases also, be expended on entirely different organs and tissues from those which are affected by the disease, and that such a want of all correspondence or adaptation, must of necessity imply a total want of all curative agency.

In regard to the third relationship, namely, that of similarity it is evident, when in any given case, a medicine is administered which is known to be capable of producing on the body, a condition similar to that of the disease, that the two forces, namely, that of the natural disease on the one hand, and that of the artificial drug disease on the other, must, on the ground of their similarity in kind and place of action, come in direct contact with each other. The result of this is, that a reaction of the vital powers takes place in the very seat of the disease, and this reaction being the opposite of the primary action, is nothing less than a reaction in favour of health—in short, a return of healthy action, and by sustaining this reaction for a time by a proper reception of the curative remedy, the disease is entirely removed, and healthy action permanently established. It is this word reaction that explains the matter. When the symptoms of the medicine are the opposite to those of the disease, the reaction, being always the opposite of the primary action, must be an action in favour of the disease, as so well tended to establish it in the system, even though its primary action has for a little, an apparently opposite effect. Even so, when the symptoms of the medicine are similar to those of the disease, the reaction being always the opposite of the primary action, must be an action in favour of health, and will tend to establish health in the system, notwithstanding that its primary action seemed to have an opposite effect. This is the relationship between medicine and disease, which constitutes the basis of the homœopathic system.—This is the spirit of the homœopathic law. We invite you to study it and examine it with the strictest scrutiny. Do not, however, connect it with any of its accidental accompaniments, subordinate appendages, and it may be useless incrustations, examine the grand primary essential principle by itself, in the light of observation and facts.

In still further establishing this point, we would appeal to well ascertained and indisputable facts, and submit these to an examination, both analytical and synthetical. On making a collection of all the authenticated cases of cure that we can find, which during the past two thousand years, have been effected by the use of one medicinal agent, or, in which the cure could in each case be distinctly traceable to the use of one agent; and making a comparison between the medicinal properties of these different remedies, so far as we at present know them, and the symptoms of the disease which they each severally cured, it is truly remarkable that, in so far as this examination has been made, the relationship of similarity is most distinctly pointed out; and not that of contrariety as advanced by the old school. And, further, all the medicines which are at present recognized by the old school to have a direct and undoubted curative effect in any given disease;—the so called specifics for example, are found to possess the same relationship of *similarity* to the disease they cure. This has been most significantly pointed out over and over again.

Again, there are now, not one or two merely, but thousands of highly-educated physicians in all parts of the world, who give their testimony that, when guided by this relationship of similarity alone, they select a remedy for any given case in which this relationship exists, they are successful in effecting a cure with that remedy. Every homœopathist is guided by this relationship every day in the choice of his remedies, and every one can attest to the success of such a mode of practice in effecting cures. We have then, first, the deduction of the principle of similarity from the analysis of recorded facts; and second, we have the reproduction of similar facts by acting upon this principle. What evidence could be stronger than this. Had there been only one or two facts to corroborate either of these points, or only one or two observers, there might have been some room for doubt; but when there are millions of facts in the form of cures effected, and thousands of observers, who could not possibly be supposed to be all mistaken, the evidence becomes most conclusive.

But further, the first allopathic authorities are now agreed, as to the necessity of making experiments with drugs on persons in health, in order to find out their pure medicinal properties. No experiments of this kind deserving the name, have hitherto been made by allopathists; so that at present, they are almost entirely ignorant of the pure medicinal properties of the drugs they are daily in the habit of using. But supposing that properly conducted experiments of this kind were made, and the medicinal properties of several drugs ascertained by them for the first time, what use could they make of such information? how would they know how to make use of the various symptoms that each of the remedies produced? To use them on the principle of *contrariety* would be impossible, perfectly impossible. Supposing the medicine produce as one of its symptoms, pains in the head as if it would burst; what use could they make of that in practice? What is the opposite of a pain in the head as if it would burst? We never hear of such a state as a feeling of pleasure in the head as if it would be crushed together. Or supposing it produced "burning or inflammation of the eye;" or "a pain in the stomach;" or in fact any other kind of pain; what use could they apply it to? The truth is, the principle of opposition or contrariety cannot be carried out in practice; there is no opposite state to a pain in the head, in the stomach, or to any other kind of pain. There is only one way in which these symptoms can be made use of in practice. The fact that a medicine has the power of acting on any particular organ or tissue of the body, shows that that medicine ought to be used in affections of that particular organ or tissue, and not in affections of such organs or tissues upon which the medicines does not act at all. And further, as it is not possible for any medicine to produce the *opposite* of any of all the thousand pains and aches to which mankind is liable, it follows that, in any given case we are to make use of such a medicine, as is known to possess the power of producing in the body, a condition *similar* to that of the disease.

But some objector may say, we care not about principles nor relationships; it is facts we want. Very well, we grant that facts are great and stubborn things, and it is mainly on the ground of facts that homœopathy has made such mighty progress. Many can appreciate the force of facts, who cannot so easily comprehend the force of reasoning on first principles. With them, and we take the great bulk of the public to be included in that class, the facts in connection with homœopathy are everything in the matter. But not so with the practitioner and those who are interested in the advancement and full development of the system. An individual that has been cured of any disease, is more interested about the *cure itself*, than about the *way* in which it has been accomplished. But the chief consideration ought to be, *how* is such a cure to be repeated?—how are we to make other cures? We cannot take this case, and act upon it as a precedent in others. Diseases, constitutions, and circumstances differ so much in individual cases, that precedents in that sense there can be none; and to be guided by such a principle would in reality be no better than chance work. The orthodox practitioners have been very much guided by this doctrine of precedents, but the consequence is, a world of confusion and contradiction. Dr. S. tried such and such a medicine for such a complaint, and found it very successful. Dr. C. has also tried it extensively in the same complaint, and found it of no use. Professor C. strongly recommends such and such a medicine in such a complaint, but Professor A. has also tried it, and found it most injurious. And so in regard to every medicine given on this ground. We will give you proofs of this by-and-by. The only certain and trustworthy course is, to be guided by that principle which has led us and led others, to the choice of the proper curative medicine in numberless cases before. That convenient and easy mode of practice drawn from precedents, if followed by homœopathists, would ultimately destroy the system, as it would then differ little from allopathy. We must, if we wish to be really successful in curing safely and thoroughly, be guided entirely and constantly by the curative relationship and not depart from it. It costs the practitioner much labor and close study, but his patients reap the reward of these.

It is truly astonishing, not only that medicine should have been so long practiced, but that it should still, in this enlightened age, be practiced by men who are not only not guided by any fixed, definite principle in choosing their medicines, but who are at the same time almost entirely ignorant of the medicinal properties of the drugs they use. No wonder that medical men have so little faith in medicine—that there is so much diversity of opinion among them in regard to the treatment of any one disease, and that such diversity of treatment should lead to such unsuccessful results.

In every department of nature we find law and order. All the various phenomena which we observe, both in the arts and sciences, are the natural expressions of certain definite laws or principles, in harmony and in accordance with which all their varied phenomena take place. There is nothing fortuitous or irregular. The very winds and storms, with all their apparent caprice and disorder, are regulated by certain well-known principles, which the skilful mariner knows how to take advantage of. The starry orb of heaven, with all its apparent confusion and disorder, is controlled and guided by a constant and fixed law; which, when understood and applied, shows all this sparkling throng in perfect order and regularity, each moving in its own sphere, in beautiful harmony with all the rest. Matter tends to matter everywhere in harmony with a law, the expression of which is the same all over the world. And so of motion, atomic attraction, chemical combination, the expansion of steam, electrical phenomena. All these occur according to well-known fixed and definite laws, each being certain and infallible in its own sphere. The dyer mixes his ingredients in certain fixed proportions, and the same hue is brought out now, that was a century ago. The steamboat pushes its course across the wide Atlantic to an hour. The locomotive wends its way along the rail to a second; and the deadly shell bursts over a given spot two miles distant, because the laws which regulate the expansion of steam and powder, and the falling of bodies being known and acted upon, are found to be invariable.

The astronomer, guided by the fundamental law or principle on which his science rests, can foretell new phenomena and facts not previously observed, as necessary results of that principle. The sailor trusts his life and fortune to the steadiness of the needle, and is not deceived—The merchant trusts a message to the electric telegraph which if wrongly transmitted might ruin him. In fact, turn where we will, and we have law and order. Some of these laws are very obvious and easily discerned, and doubtless there are many more unknown to us. And is the art of medicine—the curing of the sick, the most important and vital of all others, the only science for the guidance of which no law nor principle has been provided ?—Is this the only department of nature in which utter disorder and confusion was intended to reign, in place of order and harmony ?—Never, never. There is a law of healing—a law for the curing of disease, which when known and implicitly followed, will not deceive nor disappoint us. Without a knowledge of this law, the physician is set adrift on the public with a parchment license in his pocket, but without a compass; and the great misfortune is that, it is not himself merely that he is in danger of making shipwreck of, but the lives of hundreds, nay, it may be thousands who commit themselves to his care.

CHAPTER VI.

OBJECTIONS AGAINST HOMŒOPATHY.

Contradictory nature of—Homœopaths cure by imagination and by attending to diet and regimen—Homœopaths few in number—Homœopathy, if true, would have been sooner discovered—Some homœopathists have recanted—Homœopathy denies all the laws of physic and chemistry—The killing and curing powers of medicine—The small doses—These doses do not constitute homœopathy—Different degrees of susceptibility—Homœopathic remedies prepared to suit these—The dose must vary according to the effect to be produced—Dangerous and deadly effects of large doses—The power of small doses proved by experience—Erroneous information about small doses—Homœopathy opposed to common sense—And to the experience of the profession—Homœopathy proved a failure by Dr. Andral.

Our object will now be, to consider the various objections that are generally brought against homœopathy by its opponents. At first sight, one would think, from the great talk some would-be-learned individuals make against the system, that there were in reality a great many substantial *bona-fide* objections, but the truth is, that after we begin to examine these, almost all (that against the small doses being excepted) turn out to be mere clap-trap expedients, shifting and changing to suit every variety of character and circumstance. One day, for example, the editor of the *Lancet*, on hearing, it may be, of some individual that has died while under homœopathic treatment, will cry out most lustily, that these homœopaths, in place of giving doses of medicine which are quite harmless, do actually give dangerous and poisonous doses of the most potent drugs; and his simple-minded dupes, pleased with the statement, merely because it cuts against homœopathy, taking no thought as to its being true or false, re-echo it far and wide, hence the origin of this objection. Next day, again, while his attention is drawn to the progress of the new system, and the unprecedented success attending the homœopathic treatment, he is obliged (not being able to deny the fact), to explain them away, by maintaining that the medicine used by homœopathists is no medicine at all, and that the doses are utterly incapable of producing any effect. This, too, his credulous disciples are quite ready to swallow down, and they quickly re-echo the report—hence the origin of this contradiction.

Now what can we make of objections like these;

to maintain that the practice of homœopathy consists in the giving of large and dangerous doses of powerful drugs, and at the same time to say that, the medicine which homœopathists pretend to give is totally inert,—or in fact, no medicine at all, but only "the name;" is just flatly to contradict oneself, and to hold both to be true is a glaring absurdity; and yet this is done by many of our opponents. The redoubtable Dr. Routh, a well-known opponent of homœopathy, has pursued this very course. In one place he accuses homœopathists of giving doses of medicine so powerful and dangerous as to be sufficient to cause death, and again, in another place, in order to explain away the immense superiority of the system, as proved by an examination of statistical reports, he assumes that the medicine is devoid of all power, and the treatment equivalent to nothing at all. All prejudiced opponents take in both of these contradictory assertions as being true, and bring forward the one or the other, just as circumstances call for. The public however are not always to be deceived by expedients of this kind; expedients having the semblance, but not the reality of valid objections.

Another objector, in accounting for the greater number of cures affected by homœopathy, and not feeling inclined to retail such contradictions as the above, says, that we cure by imagination and by attending to diet and regimen. This objection, though frequently advanced is not worth the refuting, for, even supposing that the statement was true (which it is not), it is most obvious that, the objection tells most decidedly against allopathy. If we, merely by attention to diet and regimen, are able to make more, nay, even as many cures as allopaths can, does not this prove that, all their strong remedies—their bleedings, blisterings, and purgings are utterly useless? Who would not much rather be cured by imagination and attention to diet, than by bleeding, blistering, and purging? no comparison, surely. The sooner allopaths throw their physic to the dogs, and learn to cure by imagination and attending to diet, the better.

It is also said, that we have few great men in our ranks, and that our numbers are small. Some intelligent individuals have advanced this as an objection, but really we cannot see what connection it has with homœopathy at all. Homœopathy is not a system of rank and numbers, (even though in these respects it now holds a very formidable relationship to its antiquated predecessor.) The system was as true when first propounded by Hahneman, and advocated by himself alone, as it would have been even though believed in and advocated by the whole medical faculty in Europe. The circulation of the blood, when first discovered and propounded by

Harvey was just as true then, when the whole faculty was against it, as it is now, when universally believed in. Truth is truth, independent of the rank and numbers of those who are either with it or against it. The majority of the world are even now Pagans; but who would advance this as any proof in favor of paganism?

It is also objected, that if homœopathy was true it would have been much sooner discovered. This, too, is no valid objection, for, the same might be advanced against every discovery whatever. How was it that the circulation of the blood was so long in being discovered? a simple self-evident fact like that could scarcely remain long unobserved; and yet it was not till the seventeenth century, that Harvey demonstrated the true nature of the circulation in opposition to the fanciful theories of the ancients, who imagined that the arteries contained air. So also in regard to the law of attraction; people had from the beginning of the world, observed many phenomena about stones and apples falling to the ground, and thought no more of them. But, it was not till Newton, who, on observing these same facts, was enabled to rise from these to a universal law, which at once became the linking and guiding principle in all similar phenomena. And so in regard to the steam-engine, railways, and the electric telegraph. In these and all other discoveries, we ought not to decide either for or against, until we become acquainted with the facts or principles on which the discovery is said to rest; and being fully satisfied as to the truth or falsity of these, let us then reject or adopt, but not till then.

Dr. Routh and some of his followers have advanced as an objection that, some homœopathic practitioners have seen through the deception of homœopathy, and written against it. This may or may not be true. Every other system which puts the moral character of its supporters to the test, has had its recanters. The only case of the kind, in regard to homœopathy that we are acquainted with, is that of a Dr. Fickel, a German. This individual, while professing an attachment to homœopathy, was openly convicted of deception and imposture, by those with whom he professed to identify himself. The consequence was, that out of revenge for this exposure, he wrote an article, trying to prove the nothingness of homœopathy. Shortly after this, he was apprehended by the civil authorities for swindling, and put in gaol. —So much for the character of one who is brought as a witness against us. Professor Simpson in his attack on homœopathy, also introduces this case; but the truth is, that Fickel never was a true homœopath, and it is creditable to the cause, that such an individual was not able to maintain a false position in such company, but was obliged to go back to his true place.

The following objection is taken from the *Leader Newspaper.* 1st, "It," (homœopathy) "denies all "the established laws of physics and chemistry. "When anything does this, we at once call it a "delusion. It asserts, that matter of a certain kind, "increases in power as it decreases in bulk. We "know the contrary. We know the greater the "quantity the greater the power, and in exact pro- "portion. * * Also, if a man can carry only one "cwt. of coals, he never finds that by adding another, "the weight becomes lighter; it is always the con- "trary. Matter acts physically in proportion to its "quantity." This is the physical law, which according to our objector, homœopathy denies. How the gentleman came to make such a discovery as this we know not; but we must compliment him on it; as to us it is something perfectly new. Perhaps by the same process, he will discover that homœopathy denies that a pound of feathers is as heavy as a pound of lead. It is evident, that our objector entertains entirely wrong views in regard to the nature of *power;* he confounds it with that of mere *physical weight.* The power of a razor to cut is not increased, by increasing the thickness of its edge; although it would weigh heavier. But his peculiar notions about power will be better seen when we take his second objection. "2nd, Chemically, a drop "of sulphuric acid makes a pleasant draught, if put "into a tumbler of water; but use much and you are "killed, use more and you are made into a cinder. "The more used, the more determined the result. "How can it be otherwise?" Aye, how can it be otherwise? But, if there is any truth at all in our opponent's objections, it ought to be otherwise; for, mark how the gentleman confounds things that entirely differ, and destroys his own position. The *power* of one drop of sulphuric acid in a tumbler of water is, to afford a "pleasant draught;" very good, we do not deny it, but, according to objection number one, the addition of five drops ought to afford a draught five times more pleasant, and ten drops, a draught ten times more pleasant; and so on, the more you add, the more pleasant the draught. But is this true? Certainly it is not; for, our objector states, and we most fully agree with him that, in place of the power of the small dose, in affording a pleasant draught, being increased by increasing the quantity of the material, it has not the *same* power at all. In fact it *loses its power* of affording a pleasant draught altogether, and acquires an entirely different power—namely, that of *killing*. This is a point of very great importance, and one on which we have all along insisted when dealing with our allopathic opponents, that, while a small dose of any remedy when properly given, may exercise a *beneficial* effect upon a patient, that is no reason to expect that a dose double the weight of the first, should have an effect doubly beneficial. The evidence of facts is entirely opposed to such an expectation. There is a mighty difference between killing and curing: from being burnt to a cinder, and from being made whole. So is there also a wide range between the small dose that cures, and the large dose that kills. Allopaths make a boast of using large doses, and many of them often give monstrous doses, such as prove directly fatal. In fact, such cases are by no means of rare occurrence. This is not to be wondered at, when we consider that allopaths hold such opinions as those advanced by our objector. One grain of a drug is capable of doing some good; five grains will do five times more good; ten grains will do ten times more good; fatal doctrine! You that are partial to the large doses, take warning from the statement of our objector; there is such a dose as will kill, and there is such a quantity as will burn you to a cinder; but rest assured that, the curative dose does not lie near the confines of either the one or the other.

We will now consider that most common of all objections advanced against homœopathy—namely, that of the *small doses.* Our adherence to, and advocacy of these, has exposed us to the ridicule and abuse of a vast number of professional and lay opponents. It is a mighty obstacle in the way of our progress; we know that. But, being convinced by our own experience and observation, as well as that of thousands of other practitioners who have put the subject to the test, that these small doses are the most successful in the curing of disease, and therefore, the best for the patient, we advocate and defend their use. Apart from this great superiority in the curing of disease, what interest could we have in giving the small, in preference to the large doses? what possible advantage can it be to us? we know of none. The great disadvantage of the small doses, is most apparent from the great opposition manifested against them: in fact, up till now, they have been the opprobrium and bugbear of homœopathy everywhere.

Many who have heard of homœopathy only from our opponents, and are entirely indebted to that source for anything they know, or think they know of it, imagine that the system consists merely in the exhibition of small doses of medicines; now this is a great mistake. However important the small doses may be in bringing about the speedy and remarkable cures, homœopathy itself is not to be confounded with these doses. No one is a homœopathist in any sense, no matter how small his doses may be, unless he at the same time chooses his medicine on the ground of its homœopathic relationship to the disease; and every one is a homœopathist, just in so far as he is guided by this relationship in the choice of his remedies, no matter how large or small the dose may be.

Different individuals have different constitutions, some are exceedingly sensitive to external impressions; others are the very reverse. Some are exceedingly excitable; others are the very reverse. Of these again there are a great many shades, varying in intensity. Each of these too, when under the influence of any particular disease, is affected in a way peculiar to itself. So also is there a very marked difference in the effects of remedial agents on these different constitutions. On this account there is a great variety in the preparation of our remedies in order to suit the various shades of constitutions, and the various degrees of intensity of disease. In the homœopathic system, there are medicines varying in strength from the most highly attenuated drop or globule, down to the lowest trituration and mother-tincture of the raw drug. The success of the practitioner does, in many cases, depend entirely upon the selection of the most suitable dose, even after he has found the proper medicine. The repetition of the remedy too, has a great deal to do with the success of the treatment. The truth is, that the most appropriate dose of any given medicine, is not such a simple matter as some people imagine; much remains to be learned on this point.

The dose of any medicine must vary according to the particular object the prescriber has in view—according to the effects he wants to produce. Supposing an allopath was to give a drug, not to burn the patient to a cinder, nor yet quite to kill him, but to affect the system so powerfully as would just fall short of the killing effect, it is evident that the dose must of necessity be large. It is often difficult just to hit the precise quantity for this nice practice, as we frequently hear of patients being killed by such doses. But if it is desired to produce only one or two of the poisonous effects of the drug, say purging or vomiting, then the dose need not be quite so near the killing point, but still it must be sufficiently large to bring the system under the poisonous influence of the drug. Let us take mercury as the medicine, and suppose for example, that our object is to produce salivation, just suppose this, for in practice homœopathists neither give mercury, nor any other medicine to produce salivation, how much would we give for a dose? If we had no experience of our own on this point, we ought certainly to be guided by the advice and experience of those, who had been long in the habit of using that drug to produce that effect. And so we would give such a dose, and at such intervals, as had been in the experience of others found to be sufficient for that purpose. Then again, if we wanted to give mercury to act as a purgative, we would certainly, in the absence of sufficient experience of our own in this matter, be guided by the experience of those who had been in the habit of using the drug to produce that effect; and give the dose they had found to be most suitable. In the same way, if any one wanted to administer any medicine on the homœopathic principle, he ought, in the event of his having had no experience in that way himself, to be guided in selecting the dose of the medicine by the advice and experience of those, who had been long in the habit of acting on that principle. This is the course which reason and common sense alike point out for one to follow.

Allopaths having had *no experience* whatever in the use of homœopathic medicines, are not qualified to decide upon the proper dose of such medicines, neither have they any right to object to the doses employed by homœopathists, until they *condescend* to try them properly. Hahnemann himself, even after he had discovered the homœopathic law, was entirely ignorant of the power of the small doses; (no such doses having been used before his time,) accordingly, being guided by what he had formerly learned from experience, he gave his medicines in doses quite as large as those generally employed by the old-school doctors. He soon found, however, that such doses were by far too large—that they often produced very serious consequences, and on this account, he gave smaller doses. By a process of preparation discovered by himself alone, he gradually reduced his medicines to that form in which they are now generally given. These small doses are adhered to by homœopathists, because they are found to be the best that have yet been tried; should a better be discovered, we will gladly give them up.

The homœopathist never prescribes a medicine with the object of producing any of the poisonous, artificial effects of the drug. His only object is to give such a medicine as will act on the diseased part, and in such a quantity, as shall suffice to bring about a natural reaction of the system against the disease; and such a medicine he prescribes, in such a form, and at such intervals, as shall maintain the reaction sufficiently long to destroy the entire malady. In disease, the part affected is far more sensitive than it was when in a state of health, and far more easily affected by external influences. A very small amount of the natural stimulus, light, acting on an inflamed eye, causes severe pain; and in many cases any degree of light at all is intolerable; whereas, a sound healthy eye, is not in the slightest degree affected by the broad light of day. Even so, if in any disease, a medicine be given, which is capable of acting on the part affected, and that in a way similar to the disease, it is evident that, the sensibility of the part being very much excited, a very minute quantity of the medicine indeed, will materially affect the diseased part. This we would reasonably expect, and experience establishes the fact. In the present state of our knowledge of the remedial powers of medicines, it would be wrong, dogmatically to say, what ought to be the highest, or what ought to be the lowest potency in which any medicine should be used. In this matter we must be cautious in adopting any one-sided views. Two things are at present certain, namely, that the large doses used by allopaths are not only unnecessary, but that they are highly dangerous, and often attended with fatal consequences; and second, that doses infinitely smaller than those used by allopaths, when properly applied, are most efficacious in curing disease, and also, entirely free from danger. Medical literature abounds in instances of patients being poisoned by allopathic doses of medicines, though a fraction of the reality on this point, never comes to the light of day. The *Medical Gazette*, startled by an examination of this subject, makes the following statement. "We could present," it goes on to say, "rather a *serious tragedy*, if we were to collect *all the cases of poisoning* by huge doses of powerful medicines, by the disciples of this physician, and of sanguinary homicide by the imitators of that bold surgeon, though they may both enjoy high repute." The doctor gives his physic; patients die. And what often passes off as a case of natural death from disease, is nothing less than a case of poisoning from over-drugging.

But even small doses of certain substances are very often productive of serious results, as the following letter, writen by an allopath, Wm. Herapath, of Bristol, proves. "To the Editor of the *Times*—Sir, your number of yesterday, in some remarks upon Mr. Scoffner's patent for purifying sugar by sulphurous acid, left the public in doubt, as to what quantity of *lead* might be taken by human beings without injurious effects. Some time since, in the west of England, a river, the water of which had been used from time immemorial by the inhabitants of a village on its banks, without injury, was found to affect their health. Symptoms of indigestion abounded, with loss of flesh and appetite, and there were some few cases of colic; they believed that it arose from the river water, and those who used water drawn from a spring at some distance, were not so affected. I was requested to analyze the river water, and found in it 1,500,000th part of *carbonate of lead*, which arose from a mine which was worked at the distance of three or four miles from the village, on the other side of a range of lime-stone hills. Your paragraph leaves it doubtful, whether one and a quarter grains of *lead* taken in a week, would be injurious. *In the case I relate, there would be only one grain in nine gallons of water, and yet the health of the neighborhood was seriously affected.*" When such a very small quantity as this, was capable of producing such injurious effects on individuals in perfect health, is it to be wondered that, equally small, or even smaller quantities of medicinal agents should, when properly applied produce a beneficial effect on individuals in a state of disease? In every department of nature, there are numerous examples of so-called infinitesimal quantities of various agents, producing the most astounding, and often fearfully fatal results. Look at the potatoe miasm—the Indian jungle miasm—the Pontine marsh miasm—or that of cholera, measles, or small-pox. Who ever weighed or determined the quantity of any of these subtle agents which is capable of producing their respective diseases? Who can say in regard to any of them, that this or that is the smallest quantity that can produce any effect? Who ever saw or weighed the amount of material that rises from a flower in the form of odour? and yet who denies its presence and its power on that account?

No *à priori* argument or reasoning from analogy can satisfactorily establish the value of the small doses used by homœopathists. The only perfect and infallible test of their efficacy is, in their power of controlling and curing disease. We have evidence from thousands of practitioners, in all parts of the world, who have over and over again observed the unmistakable power of these doses, in arresting and curing the most rapidly fatal diseases that exist. And this is the test we wish our opponents to try it by. Many of these not being able to shut their eyes against the fact that we are more successful with the small, than they are with the large doses, have begun to use some of our medicines, and that with success; while at the same time they are giving much smaller quantities of their allopathic mixtures. These are good omens, and we rejoice to see them; but, until the law or principle of homœopathy be properly understood and acted upon, any change in the doses they administer, will be a matter of secondary importance. The small doses naturally spring out of the homœopathic law of relationship. Professor Jorg, an allopath, makes the following remark on this point:—"Medicines operate most powerfully upon the sick when the symptoms correspond with those of the disease." And of this he gives several instances; after which he adds, "yet why should I occupy time in adducing more examples of a similar operation of medicines, since it is in the very nature of the thing that a medicine must produce a greater effect when it is applied to a body already suffering under an affection similar to that which the medicine itself is capable of producing."

We shall close this part of our subject, by giving a specimen of the false and erroneous information, which our opponents spread in regard to the small doses. In an article in *Chambers' Journal* for 23d June, 1855, the author by way of giving his readers information regarding the small doses used by homœopathists, thus delivers himself: "Take a grain of aconite, for example, and mix it up with a certain quantity of water; then take a drop of this water, and diffuse it through a similar quantity of pure water; then let a drop of water again be diluted in like manner; and so on for *thirty* times, in which case, it is arithmetically demonstrable, that you have that original grain diffused through a mass of water many millions of millions of times larger than the whole earth." We take this as a fair specimen of the *kind* of information that is given to the public by our opponents, on subjects connected with homœopathy. It is not abusive, neither is it disrespectful, but it is monstrously untrue. It bears out that, when one grain of aconite is diluted *thirty* times, the whole mass of water in which the grain is so diluted, is many millions of millions of times larger than the whole earth. The author says, it is arithmetically demonstrable, that this is the case. Let us see what simple arithmetic says to it. Thus—take one grain of aconite, and mix that in ninety-nine drops of water;* take one drop of that mixture, and mix it in another ninety-nine drops of water, go on in the same manner for *thirty* times; and query how much water there is in the thirty mixtures? The author in *Chambers' Journal* says, it is arithmetically demonstrable, that you have the one grain diffused through a mass of water many millions of millions of times larger than the whole earth! Allopaths are accustomed to swallow large doses; but surely there must be some difficulty in getting this over. Many have a swallow large enough for anything that comes from an orthodox laboratory, and will feel convinced that it is true, merely because it is opposed to homœopathy; but surely, this outrage on their understanding, must stagger them. Unless intended as a joke, (against which we protest;) it is nothing less than an imposition on credulity itself. The truth is, (and any one can count it for himself,) the entire mass of water in the whole *thirty* mixtures, does not amount to *two gills!* and yet a special pleader against homœopathy, will have the audacity to say, that it amounts to a mass many millions of millions of times larger than the whole earth!! After this we are prepared for anything, no matter how grossly absurd. O, the miserable trash that allopaths are served with, by way of information on

* Homœopathists do not employ water in the preparation of their medicines.

this important subject;—when will they break down the barriers that shut out the light of truth, and shake off the trammels that bind them to an old and worn out system.

In a letter issued by the Brighton Medical Association, condemnatory of homœopathy, there are three assumptions brought forward, as objections against the system. First, homœopathy is 'opposed to common sense;' second, it is 'opposed to science;' and third, it is at 'variance with the experience of the profession.' We should have liked exceedingly to have got a specimen of the logic by which the first two of these objections were substantiated; the association, however, found it much more convenient to assume than to prove the objections. We shall meet these assumptions in a very few words; first, that homœopathy is opposed to common sense. This is a very captious statement, and one very generally advanced by our opponents; no less a personage than Professor Simpson makes use of it. We shall not enter into the philosophical meaning of the term common sense, but, shall take what, if you please we shall call a more common sense view of the objection. If the gentlemen of the association mean that, homœopathy is opposed to the common sense of those who are either entirely *ignorant* of the subject, or who possess most erroneous notions thereupon, then, we doubt not, they are right, and they are welcome to make the most of the fact. But, if they mean, that homœopathy is opposed to the *common sense* of those who *understand* the subject, then, we must beg to differ from them, and demand the proof. We can point to hundreds, nay to thousands of highly educated and talented physicians, who after studying and becoming acquainted with the system practically, (the only way to know it properly,) have found and declared it to be true. We can point to thousands, nay to millions of the laity, who, after testing the system as to its practical worth, have found it to be true, and therefore we maintain, and justly so, that the common sense of *those* who *alone* are qualified to give an opinion, is in favour of homœopathy.

Second, they say that homœopathy is opposed to science. To what kind or department of science homœopathy is in any way opposed, we are at a loss to discover; and the gentlemen of the association thought it the wisest policy not to enlighten us on this point. The only scientific truth that any objector has brought forward as being opposed to homœopathy, is contained in the objection of the correspondent to the *Leader Newspaper*, at page 83, to which we refer the reader.

Third, they say that homœopathy is at variance with the experience of the medical profession. In this we believe they are in one sense right, and to this we must plead guilty. But, the experience of the medical profession, what is it?—To what has it attained? Let the talented Sir J. Forbes give the answer, "What difference of opinion," he says, "what an array of alleged facts directly at variance with each other; what contradictions; what opposite results of a like experience; what ups and downs; what glorification and degradation of the same remedy; what confidence now—what despair anon in encountering the same disease with the very same weapons; what horror and intolerance at one time of the very opinions and practices which previously and subsequently we cherished and admired." Such is allopathic experience. And with such homœopathy is directly at variance; forbid that it should ever be anything else.

It has frequently been advanced as an objection by medical men, that homœopathy was tried in Paris by Dr. Andral, and found to be a failure. Now it is quite true that Andral did make some experiments upon fifty-four cases at *La Pitié*, in Paris, a report of which was published, not by himself, but by his clinical assistant. Dr. Irvine, of Leeds, (*British Journal of Homœopathy*, vol. 2, page 50,) has analyzed these experiments, and fully exposed their utter worthlessness, as being in any sense tests of homœopathy. The medicines prescribed were not at all suited for their respective complaints, and no one with even a very moderate knowledge of homœopathy could have made such absurd experiments. Andral we believe was perfectly honest, and did the best he could under the circumstances; but unfortunately, even according to his own confession, he never had read one of Hahnemann's works, and knew nothing about our materia medica. How then could he practice homœopathy with any chance of success? He had learned something of the new system from some French authors, sufficient no doubt to arrest his attention, but not sufficient to qualify him in putting the system to a practical and critical test.

It is now twenty-two years since these experiments were made, and at that time there was no translation of Hahnemann's writings in the French language, so that Andral was so far excusable. But what is most conclusive against his experiments, is the fact of Andral himself having, in 1851, confessed to Dr. Dunham, of New York, (*North American Journal of Homœopathy*, vol. 2, page 213, *et seq.*) that these experiments were not so extensive and accurate as the nature of the subject deserved, and he did not *now* think these experiments *conclusive*. This confession sets Andral's boasted experiments entirely aside, and whatever the gentleman may at one time have thought of them, we are satisfied that he does not *now* consider them as being conclusive against homœopathy; and neither could any other man who has any knowledge of homœopathy at all. It was Andral's failure, not that of homœopathy.

CHAPTER VII.

EVIDENCE IN FAVOUR OF HOMŒOPATHY.

The practice of homœopathy not perfect—The law is—Allopathic scepticism in regard to evidence—Testimony of Hufeland—Rau—Hartmann—Evidence from general statistics—From a comparison of statistics in inflammation of the lungs—In pleuritis—In peritonitis—In yellow fever—Value of homœopathy in violent and dangerous diseases—Allopathic speculations about the nature and treatment of cholera—Destructive nature of allopathic treatment in that disease—Allopathic treatment in favour of camphor—Homœopathy and the Board of Health—Dr. Maclaughlin's testimony in favour of homœopathy—Allopathic and homœopathic statistics compared.

In adducing evidence in favor of the truth of homœopathy, it is not to be supposed that we look upon that system as being perfect, in the sense that it is infallible. The curative relationship subsisting between disease on the one hand, and medicine on the other, being a principle or law of nature, we believe to be not only true, but perfect. The practice of homœopathy, meaning by that, the application of the principle in the treatment of disease, being entirely dependent upon the amount of our knowledge of disease on the one hand, and of the medicinal properties of drugs on the other, cannot be perfect; as our knowledge of disease and of the virtues of drugs are always increasing. In one sense, namely, that the system as a whole is harmoniously adapted to the law of cure, it is perfect; but, that it is at present so fully developed in practice, that it never can at any future time be more successful, in that sense it is not perfect. We all maintain that, while homœopathy as at present practiced is *vastly* superior to the old system; it is, by the light and guidance of scientific principles, capable of being made more and more successful in the cure of disease.

There are a great many sceptics whose minds are so thoroughly prejudiced, that no amount of evidence will be allowed to tell upon them. Upon such individuals we can hope to make but very little impression. Let Professor S. or Professor C. of the allopathic school, make any statement merely upon their own authority, and these very sceptics are ready at once to take it in, and give it implicit credit. But, let Hahnemann, or fifty, or a hundred, or a thousand of his followers state what they have in experience found to be true, and these sceptics are all incredulity together;—the statements are doubted by some, denied by others, and rejected by all. Showing that extremes of credulity and scepticism are closely allied to each other. What kind or what amount of evidence would satisfy our opponents in regard to the truth of homœopathy it is impossible to understand. No other great truth was ever ushered in with a greater amount of evidence—was ever proclaimed to the world with a more overwhelming testimony in its favour. About four thousand regularly educated physicians, in various parts of the world, have fairly and honestly tested the system; and from incontrovertible evidence, stood forward boldly in the midst of much opposition, calumny and persecution, and proclaimed it to be true. Millions of individuals of every race and clime, of every rank and condition in life—rich and poor, young and old—learned and unlearned — ministers and teachers — judges and rulers—kings and queens have been the subjects of its healing power, and all testify in its favour. What court of law could desire stronger evidence? what individual, or what body of men with unprejudiced minds could resist such evidence? And yet, our allopathic opponents, merely because the system is opposed to all their preconceived notions and prejudices, have pledged themselves to oppose it. All enquiries put to them by their simple-minded supporters in regard to homœopathy, are met, by the very convenient answer, that it is all quackery and imposture, and thus the subject is disposed of. Very different is the testimony of those who have honestly studied and understood the system. Hufeland, the Hippocrates of Germany, in speaking of the system, says, "Homœopathy seems to me to be particularly valuable in two points of view; first, because it promises to lead the art of healing back to the *only true path* of quiet observation and experience, and gives new life to the too much neglected worth of symptomatology; and secondly, because it furnishes simplicity in the treatment of disease." Hufeland was no homœopathist, but he recognized in homœopathy the evidences of a great truth.

It is a rule in allopathic practice that, the more experience a physician has in the practice of medicine, the less faith he has in it; and not a few lose all faith in it whatever. This is not the case in homœopathic practice. The more experience one has in the new mode of practice, the more he becomes convinced of its truth. Dr. Rau says, "After twenty-two years labour in this new field of science, (homœopathy) I am thoroughly convinced of its truth, and pay no attention to the uncourteous language of those blind defenders of the old dogmatisms, who would willingly crush and trample under foot the forth-coming bud of this young plant, but in vain." Dr. Hartman, too, thus expresses himself, "I have practiced homœopathy for twenty-eight years, and my practice has been very extensive. As regards the fundamental principles of our art, I can truly say, that I am more than ever convinced of their truth." Every homœopathist of any experience, could furnish testimony to the same effect, but in place of taking up more space with evidence of this nature, we shall finish this part of our subject, by an appeal to the testimony of statistics.

The following TABLE is an *Extract* from a Collective REPORT of seven European HOMŒOPATHIC HOSPITALS, up to the end of the year 1848, as published in the *North American Journal of Homœopathy*, vol. ii. page 151 :—

Disease.	No. of Cases.	Cured.	Died.	Relieved or under Treatment.
Apoplexy	21	11	6	4
Bleeding from the Lungs	138	112	9	17
" from the Stomach	11	10	0	1
" from the Womb	41	40	0	1
Burns and Scalds	53	50	0	3
Catarrh of the Chest, acute	161	158	0	3
Cough, Hooping	41	34	0	7
Cholera	59	55	4	0
Convulsions	56	40	0	16
Cramp of Stomach...	129	121	1	7
Croup	6	6	0	0
Diarrhœa	310	255	3	52
Dysentery	98	91	7	0
Erysipelas of the Face	349	337	3	9
" of the Feet and Legs ...	68	64	0	4
Enlargement of Liver	3	3	0	0
Fever, Catarrhal	304	294	4	6
" Inflammatory	58	53	2	3
" Bilious and Gastric...	1010	991	9	10
" Brain	7	6	1	0
" Typhus, (severe)	1895	1437	289	169
" " Mild and Nervous .	231	210	4	17
" Continued	294	279	10	5
" Intermittent..	1071	972	5	94
Fever, Rheumatic	399	362	0	37

Disease.	No. of Cases.	Cured.	Died.	Relieved or under Treatment.
Fever, Scarlet	102	94	3	5
Gout, (Acute and Chronic)	319	293	5	21
Inflammation of Joints, Acute	390	366	6	18
" of Bladder	8	7	0	1
" of Brain	54	25	3	26
" of Air Tubes	56	40	1	15
" of Bowels and Peritoneum	211	191	13	7
" of Kidneys	4	3	0	1
" of Liver	45	33	0	12
" of Lungs	710	629	45	36
" Pleura	371	351	5	15
" Spinal Marrow	14	13	0	1
" Spleen	9	8	0	1
" Testicles	10	10	0	0
" Throat	596	583	1	12
" Womb	15	11	0	4
" Glands	24	24	0	0
Jaundice	96	85	0	11
Insanity	23	14	0	9
Injuries, Contusions	48	43	0	5
Concussion of Brain	7	5	1	1
Lock Jaw	6	3	3	0
Measles	102	96	2	4
Small Pox	211	195	6	10
Chicken Pox	141	140	1	0
St. Vitus's Dance	11	10	0	1
Vomiting, Bilious	8	8	0	0
" Chronic	48	48	0	0

REPORT of the HALF-ORPHAN ASYLUM, New York, (a Homœopathic Institution,) from August, 1842, to 1848.

Disease.	No. of Cases.	Cured.	Died.	Relieved or under Treatment
Hooping Cough.	65	65	0	0
Diarrhœa	52	52	0	0
Dysentery...	22	22	0	0
Croup	18	18	0	0
Fever, Remittent	14	14	0	0
" Gastric...	7	7	0	0
" Brain	4	4	0	0
" Scarlet	11	10	1	0
" Typhus...	2	2	0	0
" Continued	13	13	0	0
Inflammation of Bowels	3	3	0	0
" of Lungs	7	7	0	0
" of Brain	1	0	1	0
" of Air Tubes...	1	1	0	0
" of Stomach	2	2	0	0
" of Pleura (Pleurisy) ..	5	5	0	0
" of Throat (Quinsy) ...	7	7	0	0
" of Eyes, Scrofulous Catarrhal...	255	248	0	7
Catarrh of Lungs and Air Tubes ...	92	92	0	0
Erysipelas	7	7	0	0
Concussion of Brain	2	2	0	0
Hip Disease	3	2	0	1
Consumption	2	0	0	0
Colic	2	2	0	0
Mumps	3	3	0	0
Sciatica	1	1	0	0
Cholera	2	2	0	0
Canker (Sore mouth)	9	9	0	0

Disease.	No. of Cases.	Cured.	Died.	Relieved or under Treatment
Scrofula	3	3	0	0
Scrofulous Abscesses	8	8	0	0
Eruptions, of various kinds.	232	224	0	8
Rheumatism	2	2	0	0
Jaundice	6	6	0	0
Convulsions	1	0	1	0
Marasmus (Wasting)	3	3	0	0
Total..	869	849	5	15

REPORT of the same INSTITUTION from 1848 to 1852.

Typhus Fever.	96	92	4	0
Diarrhœa and Cholera	135	130	5	0
Dysentery	86	86	0	0
Mumps.	16	16	0	0
Inflammation of the Eyes, Scrofulous and Catarrhal	156	134	0	22
Hooping Cough	21	21	0	0
Eruptions	210	180	0	30
Cholera, Asiatic	42	32	10	0
Abscesses, large...	2	2	0	0
Measles	22	22	0	0
Erysipelas -	5	5	0	0
Scarlet Fever	33	33	0	0
Quinsy	4	4	0	0
Sprains	4	4	0	0
Total	838	767	19	52

REPORT of the HOME FOR THE FRIENDLESS, in the City of New York, during the year 1851.

Disease.	No. of Cases.	Cured.	Died.	Relieved or under Treatment.
Canker (Sore Mouth)	10	10	0	0
Dropsy, General	1	1	0	0
Eruptions—Scald Head	60	54	0	6
" Itch	5	5	0	0
" Varioloid, ...	5	5	0	0
" Small Pox	1	1	0	0
Fever, Catarrhal and Gastric	9	9	0	0
" Remittent	1	1	0	0
" Scarlet	2	2	0	0
Inflammation of Eyes, Scrofulous...	44	37	0	7
" of Eyelids	7	6	0	0
" of Lungs	6	6	0	0
" of Stomach	2	2	0	0
" of Pleura	1	1	0	0
" of Tonsils	6	6	0	0
" of Knee-joints, Scrof.	1	0	0	1
Menses, Suppressed	2	2	0	0
Mumps	8	8	0	0
Otorrhœa	2	2	0	0
Ulcers of Cornea	6	4	0	2
" of Feet, Scrofulous...	7	7	0	0
Total	208	191	0	17

The foregoing statistics as a whole will stand a comparison with those of any other similar institutions; though they are by no means indices of the best results from homœopathic treatment. We will now take a comparative view of the statistics afforded by the two modes of treatment, in some of the more important diseases.

Of 909 cases of inflammation of the lungs, treated by Grisolle, Briquet, Skoda, and in the Edinburgh Infirmary, 212 died—that is about 23 per cent. or nearly 1 out of every 4. Whereas of 299 cases treated homœopathically by Dr. Fleischmann, only 19 died—that is little more than 6 per cent. or 1 in 15. Further, of 111 cases of pleuritis treated in the Edinburgh Infirmary 14 died, that is about 13 per cent. or 1 in every 8 cases. Whereas of 224 cases treated homœopathically by Fleischmann, only 3 died —that is little more than 1 per cent. or 1 in 100 cases. Again, in the Edinburgh Infirmary, out of 21 cases of peritonitis, there were 6 deaths—that is, about 28 per cent., or above 1 in every 4. Whereas, of 105 cases treated by Fleischmann, only 5 deaths occurred—that is, less than 5 per cent., or less than one in every 25 cases.* In a tabular form the figures stand thus :—

INFLAMMATION OF THE LUNGS.

	Cases.	Died.	
Treated allopathically	909	212	above 23 per cent. or nearly 1 in 4.
" homœopathically	299	19	about 6 per cent. or 1 in 1 in 15.

* Introduction to the Study of Homœopathy.

PLEURITIS.

	Cases.	Died.	
Treated allopathically	111	14	above 13 per cent. or 1 in 8.
" homœopathically	224	3	about 1 per cent. or 1 in 100.

PERITONITIS.

	Cases.	Died.	
Treated allopathically	21	6	above 28 per cent. or 1 in 4.
" homœopathically	105	5	less than 5 per cent. or 1 in 25.

In two of the most deadly scourges of the human race, namely, yellow fever and cholera, we have overwhelming evidence in favour of homœopathy; as will be seen from the following figures:—

Report of the homœopathic treatment of yellow fever in Rio de Janeiro, in 1851, by Dr. Martin, (from the *British Journal of Homœopathy* for July, 1851.)

No. of cases, 3,256. Cured, 3,029. Died, 227. Less than 7 per cent.

From New Orleans, where yellow fever raged so fearfully two years ago, we have the following report from Dr. Davis and Dr. Holcombe, showing what homœopathy could do for that disease, even in its worst form, (from the *North American Journal* for 1853, page 503.)

No. of cases, 555. Cured, 522. Died 33. Less than 6 per cent.

Under the best allopathic treatment, the mortality was from 20 to 30 per cent.

* Dr. Jewell, an allopath, gives a report from Philadelphia, of

No. of cases, 44. Cured, 10. Died, 34. Above 77 per cent.

In the *Medical Circular*, vol. ii., p. 233, we have the following report of the allopathic treatment of yellow fever on board H. M. ship Dauntless, at Barbadoes.

No. of cases, 158. Cured, 79. Died, 79. 50 per cent.

Before giving a statistical view of the treatment of cholera, it will not be out of place here, to put on record some of the views held by allopaths, in regard to the nature and treatment of that dreadful disease. It is often repeated by a certain class of medical men that, homœopathy may do very well in trifling complaints, but it will not do at all in dangerous diseases; nothing but the old system will do in such cases. We have frequently listened to statements of this kind from men who pretended to know all about homœopathy, but the truth is, it is mere talk, having its origin in pure conceit and prejudice. Recorded facts, and the experience of thousands of physicians prove, that the value of homœopathy is pre-eminently manifested in diseases of the most violent and dangerous character; and it is exactly in those very diseases, that allopathy is sure to be, not only a total failure, but to be highly hazardous and pernicious. The medicines employed, it is true, are

* See New York Journal of Medicine, vol. xii., p. 149.

strong and powerful, but they are just for that very reason the more destructive and deadly. The public is not yet sufficiently alive to the fact, that while medicines have the power to cure, they have also the power to kill. But to proceed with our record of the views and opinions of allopaths, in regard to cholera and its treatment. In the *Medical Times and Gazette*, for 8th October, 1853, we have the following passage. "After two epidemics of cholera have passed away, medical men are almost as uncertain and divided as to the most successful manner of treating the disease as they were before. Bleeding and transfusion of blood—calomel in large doses, and calomel in small—calomel alone or sometimes with opium—opium alone or combined with calomel—tartarized antimony—emetics—cold water and ice—brandy and cayenne—the wet sheet—cold bath and *Douche*—sinapisms, burnt brandy, blisters and the hot air bath—electricity, salines by the mouth or rectum—injections of salines, hot water, opium, quinine, &c.—injections into the veins—the inspiration of oxygen and nitrous oxyde—ammonia, camphor, musk, phosphorus, strychnine, essential oils, aromatics, and vegetable astringents—acetate of lead, sulphate of copper, quinine, arsenic, iron, and a host of other remedies have been tried, and the result has been a sorry one." An account of the treatment of cholera, still more deplorable than this, is to be found in Dr. Bushman's book, on "Cholera and its Cures."

All the ordinary medical theories and speculations, have entirely failed in leading to any beneficial results, in the treatment of this disease. Medicines the most potent and dangerous, have been given at a mere venture, and unfortunate cholera patients have been made the subjects of the most undisguised experimentation. One remedy after another has been brought forward and extolled, and each has in its turn been demolished by some new upstart. According to the various theories on the nature and treatment of this disease, one would imagine that the cure of cholera, was a very simple matter indeed. All these theories differ from each other, and still each one seems to have so much confidence in his own notions, that, really, provided persons apply in time, there is no room for death at all. Lately since, a writer in the *Medical Circular*, in attempting to demolish the theory and practice of some previous adventurer, (who advocated the employment of purgatives in cholera,) with the view of establishing his own pet dogma on its ruins, boldly asserts that, "astringents administered in due time, *hermetically seal up* the bowels, entirely dissipate the poison, and restore the patient to health." We have seen it somewhere recommended (whether in joke or earnest we aver not,) to plug up the anus in order to stop the discharge from the bowels; but surely this modern discovery of *hermetically* sealing up the bowels, must be by far the more effectual method.

The opinion that choleraic diarrhœa can always be effectually removed by the ordinary allopathic astringents, when taken in time, is one that very generally prevails among a certain class of the community. It is an opinion, however, having no foundation in truth, and entirely opposite to experience. Were it true, cholera as such, with all its dreadful horrors, might soon have no existence but in remembrance. Every individual would merely require to provide him or herself with a bottle of astringent cholera mixture, to be able to defy the foe. Mr. Greenhow, who had the management of the cholera patients in the borough jail of Newcastle, gives us the result of his experience in the treatment of that disease. "The notion very generally prevails," he says, "and has been much insisted, that the stage of diarrhœa can always be successfully cured by appropriate treatment. But though this is very frequently, it is by no means invariably true. In the prison some *cases of diarrhœa passed rapidly into the stage of collapse*, in spite of the careful employment of remedies which in other cases often proved perfectly and rapidly successful. My experience convinced me that the exhibition of brandy and other powerful stimulants, was not useful, and in some cases was distinctly injurious."* No better opportunity than this could possibly be found, for trying the efficiency of any particular mode of treatment. The patients were entirely under the command of the medical attendant; and the medicines prescribed, were carefully given; and still the result proves that astringents fail in curing premonitory diarrhœa.

At a meeting of the Medical Society of London, held 12th Nov., a discussion upon the treatment of cholera took place. The well-known Dr. Clutterbuck said, "He had come to the conclusion, that the employment of very active medicants in cholera, *added* to the danger; and that more persons were *destroyed* by the treatment than were saved—*if any were*—which he very much doubted. He condemned large doses of calomel and opium." †

There are many others beside Dr. Clutterbuck who believe that, numbers are destroyed by the treatment. Even the innoxious castor oil, which was introduced with some plausible prospect of success, has been found in the hands of allopaths equally unsuccessful, if not equally destructive in its results. The whole subject connected with the treatment of cholera, has now become so miserably hopeless that, the editor of the *Medical Circular*, has from an honest necessity, been obliged to confess that, "The

* Medical Circular, vol. iii, page 4ƒƒ.

† Lancet, 17th November, 1849.

subject of cholera has now merged in that of drainage, and the battle of tile drainage, *versus* stone and brick sewers, has supplanted the battle of therapeutics."* In vol. v, page 181 of the same journal, the editor thus again expresses himself. "The cause of cholera has been the *radiant bubble* which physiologists, *like children*, have pursued through all the devious paths of philosophic investigation, found everywhere yet nowhere, and vanishing like a spectre when apparently found in some earthly shape." Mr. Cox, in writing upon the treatment of cholera, says "My experience of the malady in question, during 1849, was very great; and I enjoyed very extensive opportunities of witnessing the result of various modes of treatment on a large scale." The following are some of the conclusions he came to, "that stimulants of every class and description are in the highest degree pernicious, and this in proportion to their potency, the most powerful stimulants being the most hurtful and dangerous. Turpentine was given by myself, in nine cases of which seven proved fatal, and I witnessed it administered in twenty more cases, sixteen of which resulted in death. In fact, (excepting the saline mode) it is by far the most murderous mode of treatment yet adopted or suggested."†

* Medical Circular, 13th September, 1854.

† Medical Circular, vol. iii., page 149.

Many medical men of the first standing in the profession confirm Mr. Cox's opinion in regard to the injurious influence of stimulants in cholera; and it is not, mark you, that these remedies do no good, but they are confessedly *pernicious* and *murderous* —they kill many who might recover; this is the dreadful fact connected with the treatment. What would you think of any one recommending saw-dust in cholera? not much, we presume; and yet saw-dust would actually be better than these allopathic drugs, for, though it could not possibly do any good, *murderous* it could not be, while the others are proven by experience to be so. Notwithstanding this, there are many medical men who will neither open their eyes nor their ears to learn the truth, but who doggedly adhere to old prejudiced opinions and practices. A gentleman, whose modesty prevented him giving his name, residing in a small village on the south bank of the Tay, wrote to the editor of the *Medical Circular* about his mode of curing cholera. His infallible is "tincture of ginger or cayenne pepper, made with either brandy or good malt whiskey, and given in a little warm water and sugar, with the grating of nutmeg, particularly if there is much diarrhœa present." On summing up his experience (*sic*) with the mixture, he says "I have never known it to fail."

Mr. Hunt, who had large experience in the treatment of cholera, stated at a meeting of the Medical Society of London, that " he thought cholera seldom or never checked, or at all cured,"—that is by allopathic treatment.

Dr. Priest imagines that, because chloride of lime decomposes all poisonous gases out of the body, it will destroy the poison of cholera in the body—cholera being a poison that acts only on the bowels.* The gentleman relates a case of cholera in which he imagined the chloride was successful. But in place of the medicine being given pure and by itself, (so as to secure its true action,) as it certainly ought to have been, had the gentleman had any faith in it; we find *five ounces of camphor*-water mixed with one ounce of the chloride of lime, and of this a large tablespoonful was given every half-hour. The patient to whom this was given, recovered; but had the gentleman been acquainted with the remarkable power of camphor in controlling the disease, he would never have dreamt of attributing the success of the treatment to the chloride. The camphor was undoubtedly the curative agent.

Another gentleman of the same school, in a former number of the same journal, assuming that cholera was a poison which produced a species of decomposition in the body, fancied that, as sugar was a capital thing for pickling pork, it would on the same prin-

* Medical Circular, vol. v, page 153.

ciple, cure cholera, by preserving the body from the decomposing influence of the cholera poison. This is the way that allopaths theorise about the nature and treatment of disease. This gentleman, strange to say, gave his sugar, mixed with camphor, and in practice found it successful. Ah! gentlemen, how did you come to think of giving camphor in cholera? Have you no vague recollections of sundry reports of its success in the hands of these heretical homœopathists? Do be prevailed upon, gentlemen, to take a single leaf, in place of a sentence, out of homœopathy, and rest assured you will have a more satisfactory guide in the cure of disease than you have at present. A number of allopaths, not able entirely to blind their eyes to the fact, that the camphor treatment had been more successful than any other, have employed various mixtures, in which camphor formed an important ingredient. We are glad to see good done by any means, but at the same time we lament to see that medical men will not, for reasons best known to themselves, make themselves fully acquainted with the principle on which homœopathic remedies are given, and the proper manner of giving them. Camphor, like many other of our remedies used by allopaths, is not only to a great extent prevented from exerting its true curative action, by being mixed with other drugs, but it is often used in cases in which it is not at all indicated. No one unacquainted with the principles and practice of homœopathy, can understand how, and when to use camphor to the best advantage in cholera.

We will now take a view of the results of the homœopathic and allopathic methods of treating cholera, by an examination of statistics. In doing so we must premise that, there has been no aim whatever, at any particular method in their arrangement, and as regards completeness, we have given all the statistics of any importance of which we had correct reports in our possession.

	Treated allopathically.		
In Bavaria......12,753 cases.	6,163 deaths.	$48\frac{1}{2}$ per cent.	
	Treated homœopathically.		
In Bavaria*......1,269 cases.	85 deaths.	$6\frac{3}{4}$ per cent.	
	Treated allopathically.		
In Paris...........6,543 cases.	3,374 deaths.	$51\frac{1}{2}$ per cent.	
	Treated homœopathically.		
Cincinnati, Ohio 1,116 cases.	35 deaths.	3 per cent.	
	Treated allopathically,		
Dundee Hospital...157 cases.	87 deaths.	$61\frac{4}{5}$ per cent.	
	Treated homœopathically.		
In Liverpool†...... 175 cases.	45 deaths.	$24\frac{3}{4}$ per cent.	
	Treated allopathically.		
In Stockholm.....4,143 cases.	2,447 deaths.	$59\frac{3}{4}$ per cent.	

* These cases were reported by Dr. Rath, who was sent by the king of Bavaria to collect authentic information regarding the homœopathic treatment of cholera.

† In Liverpool most of the cases were virulent, and many in a state of collapse before being seen.

	Treated homœopathically.		
In Edinburgh*	173 cases.	48 deaths.	27¾ per cent.
	Treated allopathically.		
In Christiana	2,318 cases.	1,506 deaths.	65 per cent.
	Treated homœopathically.		
In Lancaster, Torquay, and Glasgow	76 cases.	6 deaths.	8 per cent.
	Treated allopathically.		
In Helsingfors, Russia	3,328 cases.	1,607 deaths.	48¼ per cent.
	Treated homœopathically.		
In Vienna	380 cases.	49 deaths.	12½ per cent.
	Treated allopathically.		
In Copenhagen	7,515 cases.	4.047 deaths,	55⅕ per cent.
	Treated homœopathically.		
In Vienna, Moravia, Bohemia, and Hungary	1,093 cases.	95 deaths	8¾ per cent.
	Treated allopathically.		
In Paris Hospitals	4,203 cases.	3,144 deaths.	74¾ per cent.
	Treated homœopathically.		
In Russia, Austria, Berlin and Paris	3,016 cases.	264 deaths.	8⅔ per cent.
	Treated allopathically.		
In Sweden	1,165 cases.	735 deaths.	63 per cent.
	Treated homœopathically.		
In Russia†	1,270 cases.	108 deaths.	8½ per cent.
	Treated allopathically.		
In Dantzic	900 cases.	555 deaths.	61⅔ per cent.
In Berlin	1,285 cases.	832 deaths.	64¾ per cent.

* In Edinburgh, besides the disease being very virulent, many of the subjects were abandoned drunkards.

† These cases were collected from various parts of the Russian Empire, by the Consul General, Hon. Alexis Eustaphieve.

Last year, when cholera prevailed to such an extent in London, the General Board of Health, impressed with the solemn fact that, the ordinary treatment of that disease had on previous occasions been attended with woful results, issued printed forms to the various public hospitals in the city, in order to find out the exact nature of the treatment pursued in the different institutions, with the results of the treatment in each individual case. The Board intended to examine most minutely into the returns received from the different institutions, with the view, if possible, of coming to a satisfactory conclusion as to what mode or means of treatment was attended with the greatest success; and to make the result known to the profession generally, for the benefit of the public.

The result of the treatment pursued in the different hospitals, as shown by the report of the Board, was anything but satisfactory; the deaths in severe cases under the most successful treatment were at the rate of 36·2 per cent. and in some cases nearly the double of that; while, in the London Homœopathic Hospital, the deaths were only 16 4 per cent. But strange to say, the returns of the Homœopathic Hospital, which were duly sent to the Board of Health, were not included in the general report issued by the Board; and so the government and the public at large were kept in ignorance as to the relative merits of the different kinds of treatment pursued in cholera; though it was the avowed purpose of the Board to obtain and supply such information for the public good.

There is one very important fact in connection with the treatment of the cholera patients in the Homœopathic Hospital, which deserves to be extensively made known, and it is this: The medical officers of that hospital, desirous that the nature and severity of the cases received there, as well as the treatment pursued, should be witnessed and recorded by some neutral party, invited Dr. Macloughlin, a medical inspector appointed by the Board of Health, and one who was always strongly opposed to homœopathy, to watch the cases. He did so, and we cannot better convey an idea of the effect which was produced upon his mind by what he observed in the hospital, than by giving an extract of a letter, which he himself wrote to one of the surgeons of the Homœopathic Hospital:*

"You are right," he says, "I did tell you I would report to the General Board of Health the opinion I had formed of the manner the poor cholera patients were cared for in your hospital, and the success of your treatment; but finding that I could not enter into the details relative to your hospital without entering also into details relative to allopathic hospi-

* British Journal of Homœopathy, vol. xiii, page 681.

tals, which would lead me into considerations foreign to the sanitary question before me, I therefore merely gave the result arrived at in yours, along with the results arrived at in other establishments, reserving to myself the liberty to say more in detail, what is the impression on my mind as to your treatment of cholera cases, when I publish a monograph on cholera.

"You are aware that I went to your hospital prepossessed against the homœopathic system; that you had in me, in your camp, an enemy rather than a friend, and that I must, therefore, have seen some cogent reason there, the first day I went, to come away so favorably disposed as to advise a friend to send a subscription to your charitable fund, and I need not tell you that, I have taken some pains to make myself acquainted with the rise, progress, and medical treatment of cholera; and that I claim for myself some right to be able to recognize the disease, and to know something of what the treatment ought to be; and, that there may be therefore no misapprehension about the cases I saw in your hospital, I will add, that all I saw were true cases of cholera, in the various stages of the disease; and that I saw several cases which did well under your treatment, which I have no hesitation in saying would have sunk under any other.

"In conclusion, I must repeat to you, what I have already told you, and what I have told every one with whom I have conversed, that although an allopath by principle, education, and practice, yet was it the will of Providence to afflict me with cholera, and to deprive me of the power of prescribing for myself, I would rather be in the hands of a homœopathic than an allopathic adviser."

Now here is a gentleman, an allopath and an opponent of homœopathy, who had the candour, honestly to investigate the truth of the system, and with open eyes to go and witness its practical effects in one of the most deadly of all diseases, and the effect upon his mind was such, that he declared, that should he ever be afflicted with cholera, and deprived of the power of prescribing for himself, *he would rather be in the hands of a homœopathic than an allopathic adviser.* This we are satisfied is the conclusion every one will come to, who can divest himself of prejudice, and investigate homœopathy in earnest.

That the returns from the homœopathic hospital should have had no effect upon the Committee of the Board of Health, is not to be wondered at; for it has come out in correspondence that, they had previously agreed and resolved, not to publish the returns from homœopathic practitioners, for, said they, by so doing, "they would give an unjustifiable sanction to an empirical practice, alike opposed to the maintenance of truth, and to the progress of science." They had in ignorance settled that homœopathy was a delusion, and its statistics unworthy of notice. The evidence of their own medical inspector, in regard to what he saw in the homœopathic hospital, must surely have touched the conscience of some of the members of that Board.

We are surprised that the medical gentlemen, who drew out the general report, should in such a momentous matter, have allowed themselves to be so far guided by prejudice and sectarianism, as to conceal from the public, the important facts made known to them in the returns of the homœopathic hospital. Surely sectarian prejudice beclouds the reason and intellect, and shuts out the light of truth. All impartial judges would agree that, that system which saved the most lives was the system which was most in harmony with the *maintenance of truth*, and the *progress of science.* The committee appointed by the Board of Health, with Dr. Paris as its president, decided otherwise, and withheld from the Parliament and the country at large, the knowledge of the important fact that, during the prevalence of cholera last year in London, while the mortality under the *most successful* allopathic treatment, was 36.2 per cent., under homœopathic treatment, it was only 16.4 per cent.—less than one-half!

COMPARATIVE view of the two modes of treatment, taken from the Homœopathic Reports already given on the one hand, and from the Reports of the Dundee Infirmary from 1850 to 1854 on the other.

Treated allopathically.

Inflammation of Lungs 77 cases. 51 discharged. 20 deaths. 26 per cent. 6 under treatment.

Treated homœopathically.

Inflammation of Lungs 199 cases. 180 cured 19. deaths. $9\frac{1}{2}$ per cent.

Treated allopathically.

Scarlet Fever 29 cases. 23 discharged. 6 deaths. $20\frac{2}{3}$ per cent.

Treated homœopathically.

Scarlet Fever 46 cases. 45 cured. 1 death. $2\frac{1}{6}$ per cent.

Treated allopathically.

Inflammation of Brain* 10 cases. 3 cured. 7 deaths. 70 per cent.

Treated homœopathically.

Inflammation of Brain 54 cases. 25 cured. 3 deaths. $5\frac{5}{9}$ per cent. 26 under treatment.

Treated allopathically.

Apoplexy 6 cases. 1 cured. 5 deaths. 83 per cent.

Treated homœopathically.

Apoplexy 21 cases. 15 cured. 6 deaths. 29 per cent.

Treated allopathically.

Vomiting of blood 8 cases. 4 cured. 4 deaths. 44 per cent.

Treated homœopathically.

Vomiting of blood 11 cases. 10 cured. 1 under treatment.

These statistics might be easily extended if it were necessary: but we consider the above as amply sufficient. They demonstrate from beginning to end

* A disease in which strong measures are looked upon as indispensable.

the great superiority of the homœopathic over the allopathic mode of treatment; and more especially in those diseases which are allowed by all to be the most dangerous and speedily fatal. Opponents may distort and twist these figures as they please, it is of no use. The facts remain unaltered and unalterable, and speak for themselves.

CHAPTER VIII.

OPPOSITION AND PERSECUTION.

Case of Ambrose Paré—of Dr. Greenfield—Collegiate opposition to Homœopathy—And Denunciation of Homœopaths—Editorial Defamation and Slander—Dr. Combe and our opponents—Medical Directory and Homœopaths—Cause of Persecution.

It will not be necessary to advance many proofs to substantiate a fact like this, that is so generally known—namely that, homœopathists have been and are still very much persecuted and defamed by their allopathic brethren. The fact is patent to every one who is to any extent acquainted with the past history and present condition of homœopathy, either at home or abroad.

At first sight, one feels inclined to wonder that this should be the case. That one medical man, should persecute and defame his brother practitioner, who is in every respect as well qualified as himself, merely, because the latter has, to his other medical attainments, added a knowledge of a new and better system of medicine called homœopathy; and has the honesty and courage to declare his preference for that new system, and to follow it out in his practice! And yet on due reflection our wonder ceases. Almost all great improvements and discoveries which have been opposed to the prevailing customs of the age, have met with severe opposition, and the authors of them with persecution. To give only one example out of many; look at Ambrose Paré, the Father of French surgery, who first introduced the practice of arresting the bleeding from arteries arising from accident or after operation by the ligature, in place of the prevailing barbarous practice, of besmearing the part with boiling oil or hot pitch! what difficulties and opposition he had to contend against in making his discovery known! He was positively forbidden from publishing an account of his discovery; and only succeeded after years of earnest pleading in obtaining a special permit from the king directly, in opposition to the efforts of the then reigning medical faculty. The case of Dr. Greenfield too is worthy of mention. This gentleman was put in jail by the president of the College of Physicians, merely because he gave cantharides in diseases of the bladder.

In every age of the world there have been individuals or parties who, in regard to every innovation or improvement in their particular province, have felt it to be their interest to oppose and resist to the very last every such improvement; and to excite and stimulate to the same opposition all those over whom their influence extended. This has been precisely the case with allopaths in regard to homœopathy. Collegiate corporations, and educational functionaries, whose very existence were bound up with the permanency and establishment of allopathy, have felt it to be their interest to condemn and oppose that new and aspiring innovation—homœopathy; and to draw over to the same opposition the great mass of practitioners, who are ever at the beck and nod of their leaders, ready to catch up and re-echo whatever note is sounded in their ears. Those allopathic colleges and journalists, knowing the rotten and indefensible nature of the system which they have pledged themselves to teach and support; have seen with alarm the gradual rise and progress of that new and flourishing system, in the discovery and development of which they themselves have had no part nor lot; and knowing that the system differs entirely from all those time-serving and ephemeral novelties which had dazzled the eyes of the profession in bygone ages—that it is no mere addition to the old system of practice, but that, it strikes at the root of all the fallacies and imperfections of the prevailing system; and has for its aim and end the entire and final overthrow of their orthodox faith and practice; have determined to make use of every means in their power to crush this new system by force. Had they attempted to refute the claims of homœopathy on scientific or rational principles; or, to demonstrate the superiority of the old over the new mode of treatment, their course would have been in the highest degree consistent and praiseworthy. But, in place of that, they met in council and decided without even a show of reason that, homœopathy was a delusion and quackery, and its supporters were cheats and impostors. The decision harmonised with the prejudices of the profession generally, and the cry of delusion and quackery soon spread through almost their entire ranks. The mass of the laity too knowing no better, caught the infection and joined in the cry. From that moment a system of defamation and persecution of the lowest and meanest character was maintained against homœopathists, who, notwithstanding, have stood firm in the faith, and have flinched not from the cause of truth and humanity.

The medical faculties of the Universities of St. Andrew's and Edinburgh, supported by the Royal College of Physicians, resolved to refuse the degree of doctor of medicine to all students who would not pledge themselves not to practice homœopathy; and the Provincial and Surgical Association of Brighton published a manifesto to the effect, "that, homœopathy as propounded by Hahnemann, and practiced by his followers, is so utterly opposed to science and common sense, as well as so completely at variance with the experience of the medical profession, that it ought to be in no way or degree practiced or countenanced by regularly educated medical practitioners." It would have redounded much more to the honour and credit of those several bodies, had they attempted to disprove the truth of homœopathy on well established scientific principles. This, however, for a very sufficient reason they did not find convenient to do. Like their great prototype, they found it much more convenient to issue a *bull*, denouncing the new system as an innovation not to be tolerated. The system, say they, is "opposed to science and common sense," and "at variance with the experience of the profession." These are strong expressions, and heavy-like charges: and had they been proven would very properly have been highly damaging to the cause of homœopathy. But they turned out to be merely bare assertions, unsupported by even a shadow of proof. What scientific truth homœopathy denies we have never been able to find out. Surely the gentlemen might have given us one example as a specimen. The objection that homœopathy opposes science and common sense has been already considered. That it is at variance with the experience of the profession will not be wondered at when we come to examine the nature and results of that experience found in the confessions of some of the foremost allopathic authors.

The editor of the *Lancet* having taken a prominent part in connexion with homœopathy and homœopaths, we shall give a few quotations from his articles as specimens of editorial persecution. "In a series of articles," that lion of editors says, "we have endeavoured to expose the folly and knavery of homœopathy, and to make evident the sordid motives of its professors." "These men must have hearts harder than the nether millstone, and consciences seared with guilt to be able to persevere in a life of such infamy and horror. Conscious of their own falsehood, practising an admitted lie, without compassion and without remorse."

Such is the horrible language of one who is a leader and teacher in the Allopathic School. What kind of treatment can we look for at the hands of those who are under the influence and training of such a leader? The malicious ravings of this gentleman at the progress of homœopathy, though in the highest degree palatable to those of the profession, who had minds similar to his own, produced feelings of unmingled disgust in many of those who deservedly stand highest in the profession, and who were not under the influence of sectarian rancour, but were willing to extend to us the same liberty of judgment which they claimed to themselves. Not a few of these, though in no way practising homœopathy, yet, treated homœopathists as gentlemen; and, as occasion presented itself, met with them in professional consultation as brethren, notwithstanding the violent opposition of the faculty generally. This gave mortal offence to the editor of the *Lancet*, who accordingly came out with another leader in the following strain :—" We have endeavoured in previous numbers of this journal to rouse the great republic of doctors to a sense of the monstrous laxity of opinion and conduct which has prevailed in the highest quarters of the profession, on the subject of irregular practice. We have reason to believe that we have not unsuccessfully done so; that the culprits are more observant of themselves, and if not grown better, are at least more prudent. But we tell them again that mere prudence will not satisfy us; our vow is made, to extirpate without mercy this low-toned behaviour. * * * It is not easy to conceive an honest homœopath. * * * No intercourse whatever can be held—no terms must be kept with men who are slack in understanding what honour and duty so plainly require, and are willing to live under a load of obloquy and shame." In this shocking quotation we have the admission that there are men in the highest quarters of the profession who are favourable to homœopathists.

There are a number of other articles of the same venomous character, which it is not necessary to quote. It is true, that of late the editor has calmed down very much, and we no more meet with those violent expressions of storm and rage which characterise his former lucubrations. How very different from this despotic editor and his colleagues, was the course pursued by men of a truly philosophic spirit. Dr. Combe for example in a letter to Dr. Forbes on this very point thus expresses himself. "I press all these considerations upon you, not from any particular leaning towards homœopathy, or any other new and disputed branch of knowledge, but because of the transcendant importance of cultivating science in a right spirit, and offering truth a ready and unprejudiced welcome from whatever quarter it may come. Ridicule and declamation may be rightfully employed to explode errors *after they shall have been proved to be so;* but they are most unfit instruments for the primary investigation of truth, and as such ought to be banished for ever from scientific discussion, and a candid spirit of philosophical inquiry be instituted in their room." If, in regard to homœopathy, medical men had followed the advice of Dr. Combe, how different would the practice of medicine have been at the present moment; and what a blessing it would have been to mankind. But self-interest, and a spirit of opposition dictated a very different course. If they would even now lay aside all party spirit and heartburnings and begin to study the merits of homœopathy in right earnest, a great and glorious reform in medicine would very soon be brought about. But it is just because the great bulk of medical men either dare not, or will not be at the trouble to investigate for themselves, that opposition to the cause of homœopathy still continues. That they possess an intelligent conviction of the truthfulness of allopathy and of the fallacy of homœopathy, is not true. No medical man who understands his profession ever maintained that allopathy was a true system of medicine founded on any established law of healing. No one was ever so blind as to imagine this. And no one who has studied homœopathy in such a way as thoroughly to understand it, has ever found it out to be fallacious or deceitful. The truth is that, apart from the stigma of small doses, (and on this their knowledge is excessively perverted and erroneous,) few allopaths know anything about homœopathy at all; and from the course which they have pursued it is scarcely possible to conceive of their having any consciousness of being in the possession of truth. Every one who knows that he has right on his side, feels, not only that he is impregnable against all the arts and wiles of his opponents, but that he is in possession of an instrument which must eventually triumph over and destroy all opposition. Our opponents, instead of maintaining a position of high moral confidence in the defence of their system, have stooped to the lowest and meanest position that man can occupy. They have branded us with every opprobrious and hateful name, they have heaped upon us calumny and abuse without measure. They have, in as far as they had the power, excommunicated us from all the rights and privileges of professional men, and left not a stone unturned in trying to injure our good name in the estimation of the public. They will not allow us to write in their periodicals—they have clandestinely given to their adherents garbled and most imperfect views of this great question, and debarred all free discussion and investigation. Our course has ever been the reverse of this. The pages of our periodicals are open to all; and, we hold ourselves at all times open to conviction, and ready to learn. While we are candid and faithful in the exposure of what we believe to be erroneous and dangerous to the public good, we at the same time impute to no man nor party principles which they disavow. And while we freely and fearlessly express our own convictions of what we believe to be true, we usurp no authority over those who differ from us, but invite them to hear, examine, judge and decide for themselves.

The persecuting and hateful spirit which exists

among a large class of allopaths, was painfully manifested a few years ago, when a general medical directory for Great Britain was being published. The compilers anxious to give satisfaction to the profession at large, were not quite sure as to the propriety of publishing the names and titles of those medical men who openly professed to practice homœopathy, and accordingly the mind of the profession was taken on the subject. The following are some of the answers returned to the question, 'should the names of homœopathists be inserted in the Directory?'

"No list of homœopathic *'quacks and humbugs,'* I will not have my copy if you do."

"No; unless published to warn us of all such empirics."

"No; swindlers."

"No; strike the renegades out of all lists."

"No; send them to ——."

"No; omit the names of the apostates altogether."

"No; unless you like to publish the vagabonds in a distinct list of quacks and humbugs."

There were many other answers given similar to these, but the specimens here are sufficient to show the *animus* of the men who are leagued against us. We can well afford to pity those men who could entertain and give expression to such vile sentiments; and only lament that the profession of medicine should be stained and disgraced by such members.

It is but justice to record here, and we do so cheerfully, that the answers given by those gentlemen who occupy the highest position in the profession, were of a very different stamp; and, that by the influence of these gentlemen the names of homœopathists *were* published in the Directory.

There is a certain class of men among our opponents with whom no kind nor amount of reason will have any effect. They have already made up their minds that we are wrong—that we are rebels, and they will give us no quarter. True, they have no law to punish the heretic and heterodox in medicine with death, the spirit of our times would not allow it. But still there is a species of newspaper and journal defamation—of professional and collegiate calumny—of medical society gossiping, all intended to injure our reputation and destroy our usefulness. And considering that this conduct is on our part altogether undeserved, it is not less criminal than imprisonment or banishment.

And what, let us ask, is the cause of all this persecution and opposition? Are we deficient in any of the qualifications which go to constitute the regular practitioner? No; we have gone through the same courses of study—have been educated in the same schools, and are in possession of the very same certificates, degrees, and diplomas with themselves. Are we less in earnest about the health and welfare of the community? Verily no; every one who knows anything about homœopathy, knows the great amount of toil, deep research, and close study that are required in its practice. Are we less successful in curing disease than they are? Let facts speak and examine our statistics. Is the practice of homœopathy hazardous? No; it never can be; while that of allopathy is proverbially and eminently so. Would the prevalence of our system operate injuriously on society? No; it strikes at the root of many of the abuses and corruptions of the age; while allopathy in many instances ministers to these and fosters them. Is allopathy more consistent with reason and facts than homœopathy? We invite them to the investigation and proof of the subject.

The true cause of this persecution is not to be found in one nor in all of these. It is to be found in the prejudice, self-interest and fear of public opinion, on the part of our opponents on the one hand, and in the inherent truth of homœopathy on the other. We hear of no such opposition to any other system, nor to any thing else belonging to medicine. Some medical men, it is true, class homœopathy with Holloway's pills and other quackeries of the same kin. Others again class it with hydropathy, mesmerism, and other novelties. But do any of these other quackeries or novelties meet with such opposition as homœopathy? No: none of them! And why? Medical men know full well that these will soon find their level, and cannot in any marked degree affect their craft. But homœopathy! ah, there is something in that which staggers them. It is unlike all past impositions—all ephemeral systems which have come to an early death. There is something in homœopathy which troubles and annoys them exceedingly. They now begin to see and feel that there is a vital principle in it which will prevent its natural death, and therefore, they must try to crush it by force. They will not let it alone, nor give it a fair field. Calumny, defamation and persecution must be had recourse to in order to destroy it, but all to no purpose—it lives and thrives still. Having buckled on the armour of truth we are confident of victory. We have gained much, and are conquering still; and, though we may not be inclined always to submit to the unjust persecution of our opponents, we will not stoop to throw back the sentence of exclusion or condemnation upon any. We invite and encourage all to come and join with us in the cause of truth.

CHAPTER IX.

ALLOPATHIC REVELATIONS.

Different Classes of Medical Men—Confessions of Dr. Forbes—of Bichat—Dr. Guy—Boerhaave—Gardner—Andrew Combe—Adam Smith—Dr. Routh—Paris—Professor Widekind—Hufeland—James Johnson—Franks—Reid—Krueger Hansen—Sir Astley Cooper—Keiser—Addison—Abernethy—Professor Gregory—Dr. Bailie—Dickson—Brown—Leeson—The Editor of the Lancet—The Medical Circular—Dublin Medical Journal—Medical Times.

THE advocates of the old system of practice having so violently condemned and opposed homœopathy; one would naturally expect that they would have some confidence in the system they themselves practiced—that they would have some faith in it as being a system based on true and sound principles, and therefore highly beneficial to society. One would really expect this, for it is equally true, that no system of error can possibly tend to the commonweal, however strongly it may be advocated, or however much it may appear to benefit a class; and that every system based upon truth, must contribute to the public good, no matter how much it may be denounced, or how much it may appear to injure a particular party. To say that medical men of the old school have no enlightened confidence in the practice they pursue, may be within the bounds of truth; but to say that, as a rule, they knowingly practice a fraud on the public, we do not believe to be true.

In order however, to have something like a correct knowledge of the real condition of allopathic practice, we shall take an unprejudiced view of the evidence of the profession itself on this subject.

The great mass of allopaths may be divided into three classes. 1st, Those who follow their profession merely because it is their profession—because they have learned it; who take no pains whatever to ascertain whether their practice is based on truth or error—easy-minded individuals, who are quite indifferent on the subject. There is no lack of this class. 2nd, those who are intent on making money; whose grand and only criterion of the good or the true in medicine is a lucrative practice—sharp fellows, who have generally a vocabularly knowledge of all popular systems, which they can explain, denounce, or approve of, just as it may happen to suit the "main chance." This too forms a numerous class. 3d, those who, by hard and long-continued study, have made themselves masters of their profession—men of a high intellectual stamp, guided by an innate love of scientific and philosophic research, who have carefully examined the claims of the system they practice, and narrowly scrutinized the evidences of its truthfulness. Of these there is a goodly number. And as these are the only men whose judgment in regard to the true nature of the allopathic system of practice would be worth receiving; to them we will appeal for evidence. The first of these we shall consult is Dr. Forbes, one of the court physicians, and a gentleman of European celebrity. In the *Foreign and British Medical Review* he thus expresses himself:—

"1st. That in a large proportion of the cases treated by allopathic physicians, the disease is cured by nature, not by them.

"2nd. That in a lesser, but still not a small proportion, the disease is cured by nature, in spite of them; in other words their interference opposing, instead of assisting the cure.

"3rd. That consequently, in a considerable proportion of disease, it would fare as well, or better, with patients, in, the actual condition of the medical art, as more generally practiced, if all remedies, at least all active remedies, especially drugs, were abandoned. * *

"Although homœopathy has brought more signally into the common day light this lamentable condition of medicine regarded as a practical art, it was one well known before to all philosophical and experienced physicians.

"It is in fact a truth of such magnitude—one so palpably evident, that it was impossible for any careful reader of the history of medicine, or any long observer of the progress of disease, not to be aware of it. What, indeed is the history of medicine but a history of perpetual changes in the opinions and practice of its professors, respecting the very same subjects—the nature and the treatment of diseases? And, amid all these changes, often extreme and directly opposed to one another, do we not find these very diseases, the subject of them, remaining (with some exceptions) still the same in their progress and general event? Sometimes, no doubt, we observe changes in the character and event, obviously depending on the change in the treatment, and alas! as often for the worse as for the better; but it holds good, as a general rule, that amid all the changes in the treatment, the proportion of the cures and deaths has remained nearly the same, or, at least if it has varied, the variation has borne no fixed relation to the difference of treatment." And further on while speaking on the same subject, he adds, "Things have arrived at such a pitch, that they cannot be worse. They must mend or end." Such is Dr. Forbes' estimate of allopathy.

But this is not all, at page 258–9 of the same Review when speaking of the comparative powerlessness and uncertainty of allopathic medicine, he adds, "What difference of opinion, what an array of alleged facts directly at variance with each other;

what contradictions; what opposite results of a like experience; what ups and downs; what glorification and degradation of the same remedy; what confidence now—what despair anon, in encountering the same disease with the very same weapons; what horror and intolerance at one time of the very opinions and practices which, previously and subsequently, we cherished and admired."

Ask one of the gentlemen of the second class, and what a different report he will give of the present state of medical practice. He will tell you of this wonderful discovery, and of the other wonderful discovery—of this great improvement, and the other great improvement—of this new medicine and the other new medicine: in fact, of a host of things, to persuade you that the profession has made great progress; and that medical men now-a-days are far more able to cure diseases than they used to be. The great thing with these gentlemen is, to make people believe that medical men know far more than they really do Not so with Dr. Forbes: he believes that medical practice is now in such a deplorable state, that it "cannot be worse;" and, from the evidence before us, we suspect that he is right.

The celebrated *Bichat*, after many years experience thus describes the allopathic system:—"To what errors have not mankind been led in the employment and denomination of medicines? They created deobstruents, when the theory of obstruction was in fashion, and incisive when that of thickening of the humors prevailed. The expressions of diluents and attenuants were common before this period. When it was necessary to blunt the acrid particles, they invented inviscants, incrassants, &c. Those who saw in diseases a relaxation or tension of the fibres, the *laxum* and *strictum* as they called it," (medical jargon,) "employed astringents and relaxants. Refrigerants and heating remedies, were brought into use by those who had a special regard in diseases to an excess or a deficiency of caloric. The same identical remedies have been employed under different names, according to the manner in which they were supposed to act. Deobstruent in one case, relaxant in another, the same medicine has been employed with all these opposite views; so true is it that the mind of man gropes in the dark, when it is guided only by the wildness of opinion."

"Hence, the vagueness and uncertainty our science presents at this day, an incoherent assemblage of incoherent opinions, it is perhaps of all the physiological sciences, that which best shows the caprice of the human mind. What do I say? It is not a science for a methodical mind. It is a shapeless assemblage of inaccurate ideas, of observations often puerile, of deceptive remedies, and of formula as fantastically conceived as they are tediously arranged."

Such is allopathy. In its exterior, both before and since Bichat's time, it has been ever changing; but in its real nature it has been ever the same. Dr. Guy, a living author, accounts for this sad state of things in this way. "That in health and, (by natural inference,) in disease every function of the body varies within wide limits of intensity. This fact is the key to the imperfections of medicine as a science, and to its deficiency as an art." This is a mere palliative excuse, quite in keeping with the allopathic mode of treating evils. It ignores the true root of the evil, which is entirely in the rottenness of their system of medicine, and its inefficiency to cope successfully with disease in all its varying forms. A true system of medicine ought to be capable of adapting itself to the ever varying symptoms of disease, and the changing functions of the body, for these variations and changes will ever continue to exist. It is simply ridiculous to throw the blame of the imperfections and deficiencies of allopathy upon the varying functions of the human body.

Boerhaave says, "If we compare the good which half-a-dozen true disciples of Esculapius have done since their art began, with the evil that the immense number of doctors have inflicted on mankind, we must be satisfied, *that it would have been infinitely better, if medical men had never existed.*"

The following confession of Dr. John Gardner, an

opponent of homœopathy, is of great importance, as showing the total inefficiency of allopathy in the treatment of scarlet fever on the one hand, and the successful results of homœopathic treatment on the other, he says: "In the course of many years' experience I have had many times reason to feel deeply the want of a remedy against scarlet fever. It will, I suppose, be admitted by all, that this disease is the result of a specific poison; and that the general principles of treatment, as applicable to other fevers, whether arising from aerial poisons or other causes, often disappoint us in scarlet fever. During the prevalence of this epidemic at certain seasons a more malignant character seems impressed on the disease. Our best means fail, and our patients die, apparently wholly unaffected by our treatment. Such at least has been my experience. I have seen whole families thus swept off, in spite of every effort, and the united councils of many practitioners."

This same Dr. Gardner, having at a later period been induced to try *belladonna*, (a homœopathic remedy,) in this disease, thus relates his experience with it. "Without reckoning slight cases of scarlet fever and sore throat, I have treated 30 cases with symptoms more or less grave, by means of the *belladonna*. In very many of these I should formerly have entertained no hope of seeing the patient pass through the attack, the approach of the disease being marked by a malignant aspect. I need not enumerate the peculiar symptoms which characterise fatal scarlet fever, they are well known to every practitioner. In the absence of the *belladonna* I have watched with great anxiety these fatal tokens; they allow little room for our anticipations being negatived. But with the *belladonna* I have not yet met with a fatal case." Dr. Gardner is a well known allopathic physician, one who knows his profession well; and as he has had practical experience in the subject of which he has written, his testimony is most decisive, at least in so far as his experience went. Belladonna is a well known homœopathic remedy in certain forms of scarlet fever, and its efficacy, as witnessed by Dr. Gardner, was such that he had never known it to fail, even in those cases in which he could have entertained no hope when using allopathic remedies. The efficacy of belladonna however in curing scarlet fever, is not any more remarkable than that of all the other remedies in the homœopathic materia medica, when these remedies are properly used. It is no mere accident or coincidence that belladonna cures scarlet fever. Experiments of the most satisfactory character on healthy individuals, prove beyond a doubt that belladonna actually does produce on the healthy body a diseased condition, having a striking resemblance to that form of scarlet fever which it is found to cure. And it was on the ground of its being able to produce this artificial state of disease, resembling scarlet fever, that it was first employed and recommended by homœopathists in the treatment of that malady; and its successful results in practice prove the truth of the principle which first lead to its use. There are certain forms of scarlet fever for which belladonna is not suited, but every true homœopathist knows how to select the proper remedy for every form of the complaint.

The highly accomplished Dr. Andrew Combe on reviewing the present condition of medical practice was constrained to make the following confession. "In fact," he says, "medicine as often practiced by men of undoubted respectability, is made so much of a mystery, and is so nearly allied, if not identified with quackery, that it would puzzle many a rational onlooker to tell which is the one and which is the other." Dr. Combe was well known to be a most accurate observer of facts, and a most highly talented physician; his evidence is therefore valuable.

Another authority of almost equal importance, namely the well known Adam Smith, makes a confession nearly to the same purpose as Dr. Combe. He says, "The great success of quacks in England has been altogether owing to the real quackery of the regular physicians."

The following statement of Dr. Routh of London shows the deception that is practiced, and affords an instance of the loose and vague language employed by allopaths. He says, that some of his "*most remarkable cures*" were effected by *bread pills!* Now, for any one to believe that he has cured a disease with bread pills, is simply to believe an untruth. Bread is an alimentary, nutritive substance, and is no medicine; it has a nutritive and not a medicinal action on the organism. The confession of Dr. Routh is however an important one, though we by no means approve of the practice of deceiving a patient by palming bread pills upon him in place of proper medicine; still, the more of the *remarkable cures* the better, and certainly the more bread pills, and the less allopathic drugging, the better for the public. We would hear of more remarkable cures, if allopaths generally would abandon their physic, and give instead Dr. Routh's bread pills.

In speaking of those horrid mixtures which allopaths are daily in the habit of prescribing, Dr. Paris says; "The file of every Apothecary would furnish a volume of instances where the ingredients of the prescription were fighting together in the dark."

Professor Widekind, an opponent of Homœopathy, says: "In our present mixture practice we may get grey, and if God pleases, white hair, but never experience. If, however, Homœopathy induces us to give *less medicine, to change it less frequently, and not to mix many drugs together, we may some day, with careful observations, glory in medical experience which we unhappily cannot do at present."—Hufeland's Journal*, 1828.

And that the public would upon the whole be benefitted by a total abandonment of every allopathic medicine whatever, we have the testimony of no less an authority than Dr. Hufeland, of Berlin, he says: "My opinion is, that more harm than good is done by physicians; and I am convinced, that, had I left my patients to nature, instead of prescribing drugs to them, more would have been saved." This strengthens Dr. Routh's evidence, in favour of bread pills. How would the great mass of allopathic physic takers feel if a law were passed, entirely prohibiting the use of all kinds of drugs, and nothing but bread pills to be used in stead? What would the opium eater do, when he had neither opium, nor morphia, nor laudanum to flee to? What would the pill-consumer do, when all his pills were taken away, and he had neither salts nor senna, nor jalap to betake himself to? What would the tonic and stomachic mixture drinker do, when his quinine was gone, and no bark, columba, quassia, nor ginger was to be got? How would these and a thousand others relish the bread pills, in place of their accustomed dose of orthodox physic? We fear they would think it was all up with them, that they could never survive without drugs. And yet the evidence of Dr. Hufeland, Dr. Routh, and others would lead us to believe that the change to bread pills would be for the benefit of the sick, more patients would be saved, and more remarkable cures effected.

Dr. James Johnson also corroborates this in the following terms: "I declare," he says, "it to be my most conscientious opinion that, if there were not a single physician, or surgeon, or apothecary, or man-mid-wife, or chemist, or druggist, or drug in the world, there would be less mortality amongst man-kind than there is now." These are startling statements and we can conceive of no motive whatever these gentlemen could have in giving expression to them, but a sincere conviction of their truth. We have testimony from the allopathic camp that, there is something more dreadful than this still in connexion with allopathic practice.

Frank says, "The medical police, is restricted to public business, and directed against contagion, epidemics, quacks, &c. But it is not considered, *that thousands are slaughtered in the quiet sickroom.* Government should at once, either banish medical men and their art, or, they should take proper measures, that the lives of people may be safer than at present, when they look far less after the practice of this *dangerous art, and the murders committed in it, than after the lowest trades.*"—*System der Mediz. Poliz., vol. i.,* 6.

Dr. Reid too makes the following horrifying confession. "More infantile subjects," he says, "are perhaps, diurnally destroyed by the mortar and pestle than, in the ancient Bethlehem, fell victims in one day to the Herodian massacre."

The well-known Sir Astley Cooper too, bears testimony on this subject in language not to be misunderstood. "The science of medicine," he says "was founded on conjecture, and improved by murder."

"I know very well," says an old practitioner, "that perhaps more than seven-tenths of mankind die, *not from disease, but from the unsuitableness and excess of medicine."—Algem. Anzeiger. d. Deuschen*, 1833, 235.

Keiser says, "In most cases, the proverb is true, that the remedy is worse than the disease, and the doctor more dangerous than the disorder."--*Syst. der Mediz.*

Though the great mass of the public have never dreamt of the horrors connected with allopathic practice, there have always been a few who knew them well. Among these, we cannot but here refer to *Addison*, who, in a number of the *Spectator*, gives a picture of the actual practice thus: "If we look into the profession of physic, we shall find a most formidable body of men; the sight of them is enough to make a man serious, for we may lay it down as a maxim, that when a nation abounds in physicians, *it grows thin of people.* Sir William Temple is very much puzzled to find out a reason why the northern hive as he calls it, does not send out such prodigious swarms, and overrun the world with Goths and Vandals as it did formerly; but had that excellent author observed that there were *no students in physic* among the subjects of Thor and Wodin, and that this science very much flourishes in the north at present, he might have found a better solution for this difficulty than any of those he has made use of. This body of men in our country may be described like the British army in Cæsar's time; *some of them slay in chariots and some on foot.* If the infantry do less execution than the charioteers, it is because they cannot be carried so soon into all quarters of the town, and dispatch so much business in so short a time. Besides this body of regular troops, there are stragglers, who, without being duly listed and enrolled, do infinite mischief to those who are so unlucky as to fall into their hands."

Abernethy says: 'There has been a great number of medical men of late years, but, upon my life diseases have increased in proportion." Professor Gregory declares, "that medical doctrines are little better than stark-staring absurdities."

Dr. Bailie declares that he has no faith whatever in medicine.

Dr. Dickson says "so far as my experience of medical matters goes, few people are permitted to die of disease. The orthodox fashion is to die of the doctor."

In case the reader should now be beginning to think that he has had a sufficiency of confessions of this sort for the present, we shall introduce here a published specimen of allopathic treatment. Professor S. H. Bennet, (an opponent of homœopathy,) in speaking of the allopathic treatment of consumption goes on to say, "Thus it is by no means uncommon to meet with patients who are taking at the same time a mixture containing *squills* and *ipecacuanha* to relieve the cough; an *anodyne draught* to cause sleep and diminish irritability; a mixture containing *catechu, gallic acid, tannin,* or other astringents, to check diarrhœa; *acetate of lead* and *opium pills* to diminish hæmoptysis; *sulphuric acid drops* to relieve the sweating; and *cod-liver oil* in addition. "I have seen," he adds, "many persons taking all these medicines and several others at one time, with a mass of bottles and boxes at the bedside sufficient to furnish an apothecary's shop." No wonder that consumptive patients are incurable under such monstrous treatment as this! how can they? It is *fashionable* with some doctors, at the present day, to give their consumptive patients *iodine* to paint over the chest. Poor deluded patients, they may just as well paint the soles of their feet.

The entire system of allopathic therapeutics, and almost the whole of their materia medica are now looked upon by men of science as destitute of all value. Dr. Brown says, he "*wasted* more than twenty years in learning, teaching and diligently scrutinizing every part of medicine." Twenty years of such study the doctor looked upon as so much time *wasted.*

Mr. Leeson, an opponent of homœopathy, thus expresses himself on the same subject. "There are," he says, "*about four hundred and ten preparations* in the pharmacopœia of the Royal College of Physicians, which no doubt are considered by that learned body as useful for medicinal purposes, or else they would not have been mentioned there. It is from this collection that the medical youths of this country are instructed to cull their remedies, and apply them in every form of disease. Now, any practical man of ten or twenty years' standing must have found that *four hundred of these preparations* are of little or no value whatever in the treatment of any form of disease; and, that about *the remaining ten* might have assisted him in reducing at one time or other, cases occurring in every department of his practice.

"Nearly all the waters, confections, decoctions, extracts, infusions, liquors, mixtures, essential oils, spirits, tinctures, have little or no influence over any form of disease, when used as internal or external remedies.

"Many of the mineral preparations are absolutely injurious in their effects under every circumstance, while the retention of other remedies is burlesque and nonsense. Why, then, divert the mind of the student by compelling him to study the natural history, preparation, properties, composition, effects and uses of such a farrago of worthlessness; while the higher and more philosophical walks of medical science are entirely kept from his grasp? Now this system must be adopted either by design or ignorance; if by the former, the person to whom the legislature have entrusted their confidence should be discharged from their several appointments with fine and imprisonment; or, if from the latter, be discharged as incompetent, &c."*

Such are the conclusions to which some of the best and foremost in the profession have come to in regard to the allopathic mode of medical treatment. The public in general know nothing of this. They see the outer garb of the profession all fair and promising; its advocates clothed with professional dignity, dispensing their nostrums and mysterious medical advice with that decision and assumption as though they had commission and authority from the veritable medical St. Peter himself. These confessions give a peep behind the scene, and reveal the hidden deformities of that wretched system.

But we are not yet finished with this head. There is a class of men who, from their peculiar position do undoubtedly exercise a powerful influence over the profession, and who to a great extent give to it its general tone—we mean editors of medical periodicals. And as most of these gentry have had a hit at homœopathy, we shall take one or two of them to task, and hear what they have to say in behalf of their own sys-

* Liebig's physiology applied in the treatment of functional derangement and organic disease.

tem of practice. The most prominent of these is the editor of the *Lancet*, we shall therefore take him first.

"The subject of specifics," he says, "briefly noticed in our last number leads us, this week, to the consideration of *empiricism* in medicine, with which the use of specific remedies has in general been intimately associated. The true meaning of the term 'empiricism' is precisely equivalent to *experimentation*, the system of making trials, in order to find out what are the facts connected with a given subject. It has been too much the custom to oppose what is called *rational* or *empirical* medicine, as if there were really anything discrepant in their nature; whereas, empiricism, is the most rational thing in the world." * * *

"The vast extent of the sciences connected with medicine, the intricacies of the inquiries which they involve; and above all, the extreme difficulty of bringing the truth of rational science into immediate and profitable relation with the phenomena of life, have conspired to render the progress of medical theory exceedingly slow; and it must be confessed that with all our science, the practice of medicine owes a very great part of its efficiency to simple experience."

"A majority of our most potent means of combating disease are derived from simple experience, and we are unable to give anything like a satisfactory explanation of their mode of action."

This expounder and teacher of medical science holds and teaches that, empiricism and experimentation are equivalent terms, and that the system of experimentation and empiricism is the most rational thing in the world. We fully agree with the gentleman that experimentation is highly, yea most rational in its own place. But where is its right place? that is the question. What is to be the nature of, and who are to be the *subjects* of our experiments? Is it the sick, the afflicted and dying, that are to be the subjects or who is it? The truth must come out: the sick, the afflicted, and the dying, are, in reality, the subjects of allopathic *empiricism* and *experimentation.* How dreadful! Wretched creatures!! No wonder that the history of medicine furnishes us with such tales of woe. How can it be otherwise? Here is a medical teacher of the first stamp advocating the practice of making the sick and the dying the subjects of empiricism and experimentation: well may the public cry out "save us from our friends!" We deny that the sick are the proper subjects of experimentation. These apply to us to be cured and not to be experimented upon.

The same redoubtable editor in one of his more calm and serious moments—free, for the time being from the dangerous heat and excitement of controversy—arrested it may be by the accumulating facts in favour of homœopathy, takes an impartial view of the miserable system which he himself advocates, and feels compelled by sheer necessity to make the following confession. "How little do we know of disease compared with what we have yet to learn! Every day developes new views—teaching us that many of what we before thought *immutable truths* deserved only to be classed with *baseless theories*; yet dazzled with the splendour of great names (authorities) *we adhere to them*. On these theories which have USURPED THE PLACE OF TRUTH, a system of *routine* or *empirical* practice has grown up—*vacilating*, *uncertain*, and often *pilotless* in the treatment of disease."

It is scarcely possible to understand how, in the face of such confessions as these, men will still continue to advocate and defend a system so deplorable. Surely it is not from a love or regard to truth or humanity; what then can it be? Reader can you understand the why? *Baseless theories* in the place of immutable truths, knowing them to be so, and still adhering to them; a *routine* and *empirical* system of practice founded on these *baseless theories*, palmed on the public *as if true*—what can we think of it? Is it not full time that an entire reform in medicine should take place? That this *routine empirical* system of *baseless theories* called allopathy, should as a system be discarded and given up?

The editor of the *Medical Circular* also makes the following confession, "We will not deny," he says, "there are many prejudices among professional men, and that stupendous folly will have a better chance of being received, if it comes from an hospital physician, than an important truth, if it be merely recommended by a modest and humble name." And further when referring to their theoretical reasonings he says, "If medical men would consent to discard their habit of theorizing, which exhibits itself in a great variety of disguises, and content themselves with a simple observation and record of facts, the profession of medicine would rapidly acquire definiteness and accuracy, and rise to the rank of an exact science." So say we; and until such a reformatory change takes place, the science of medicine will still continue to be what it is now—a mass of stupendous follies. The *baseless theories* which form the foundation of the allopathic system, must first be abandoned before any reform can take place. Homœopathy as a system, is a faithful and simple observation and record of *facts;* and that is the reason why it possesses *definiteness* and *accuracy*, (both of which allopathy wants) and therefore deservedly ranks as one of the exact sciences.

The same editor makes a fuller confession still, no further back than September last, he says, "Let the truth be honestly confessed—the practice of medicine is *empirical* to *this day*."

The editor of the *Dublin Medical Journal* is still more candid than his English cotemporaries. "Assuredly he says, "the uncertain and unsatisfactory art that we call medical science, is no science at all, but a mere jumble of inconsistent opinions, of conclusions hastily and often incorrectly drawn, of facts misunderstood or perverted, of comparisons without analogy, of hypotheses without reason, and of theories not only useless, but dangerous."

The editor of the *Medical Times* too, calmly but firmly reveals the present condition of allopathic practice in these words, "The most profoundly learned members of the profession *begin to waver about the positive efficacy* of their art, preferring in the greater number of instances to become *silent lookers on* in their attendance on the sick, rather than *hazarding the risk* of *impertinent meddling* with the grand and all-efficient workings of the human body."

CHAPTER X.

PROGRESS OF HOMŒOPATHY.

The necessity for Medical Reform—Progress of—Interest of the Public in this Reform—Allopaths must investigate Homœopathy, &c., &c.

WHO, after perusing these confessions, can have the slightest doubt that the old system of medicine is one entirely destitute of truth; pernicious and destructive in its effects, and therefore unworthy of support. These confessions are solemn legacies given to the world by men who could not be suspected of being actuated by any other motive, than a sincere conviction of the truth of what they said. They were men too, who, from their experience and position must have known their profession most thoroughly; better, infinitely better than the great mass of practitioners who are ever ready to make a boast before the public, and to hoodwink them by a display of professional lore.

The collateral branches, such as anatomy, chemistry, physiology, pathology, &c., as already mentioned, are of paramount importance, and do not in any sense or degree constitute allopathy. It is the allopathic practice of physic that requires to be reformed. It is that *routine* and *empirical* system of medication, founded on *baseless theories* that ought to be abandoned. It is altogether impossible to improve such a system, so long as it has such a foundation; and once remove the foundation, and the entire superstructure falls to the ground. That foundation of baseless theories is entirely incompatible with that simple *observation* and *record* of *facts* which is peculiar to homœopathy, and which gives it all that *certainty* and *precision* which entitle it to rank among the *exact sciences.*

That allopaths have been instrumental in doing good no one will call in question; some of their remedies, unknowingly to them, act homœopathically, and in this way occasional cures have been, and will still no doubt be effected. But, oh! who can estimate the vast amount of mischief and misery which their system has wrought in the world. The confessions given, dreadful as they certainly are, are but faint indices of the painful realities. But such a sad state of things will not, cannot always continue: they must "*mend or end.*" We believe they will mend.

A great reform called homœopathy has already begun, and is steadily going forward. Taking its origin little more than fifty years ago, in the centre of Germany, it has spread with amazing rapidity all over Europe. In Great Britain, there are seventy homœopathic dispensaries and two public hospitals. In London alone, there are 63 practitioners, and in the provinces 138. In France, there are between 400 and 500 homœopathic practitioners. In Paris alone, there are, 56.—In Vienna, 40.—In Madrid, 17.—In Berlin, 11.—In Dresden, 11.—In Leipsic, 10. Besides proportional numbers in the smaller towns all over the continent.

In Europe, there are 45 homœopathists who are Professors in Universities. 31, who are court councillors. 20, who are court physicians; and 15, who are medical councillors.

The reform has also extended itself to Asia, Africa, and America. In the latter country, homœopathic practitioners are counted by *thousands*. In the State of New York alone, there are upwards of 300 legally qualified practitioners. The reader can at once see from this short statement of progress, that homœopathy is a great fact in the world—a living reality, having a broad and firm footing; though our allopathic opponents would have the public believe that it is dead or well nigh defunct. Our good ship has been steadily progressing; already the rippling of the changing tide is seen on the waters, and our full spread sails beginning to fill with the first breeze of that favouring gale which shall carry us safely over the rugged breakers of time-hallowed custom and prejudice, and which shall leave our self-confident opponents, unless they take timely warning, on the shallows and quicksands; and like their brother alchymists of a bygone age, be compelled to administer their decoctions and elixers to the moles and the bats.

This great reform in medicine is intended to benefit the public, and not the faculty. The present system answers their individual purposes well enough, and therefore they will be the last to cry out for any change. Indeed, no system could be conceived which would answer the purpose of the doctor better than one of *routine*, *empiricism*, and *experimentation*, and therefore they will not alter a peg until forced to it by public opinion. This reform when accomplished, shall not only rid the world of an immense amount of suffering and misery, but shall greatly contribute to the well-being of the human race, both in a physical and moral point of view.

The best interests of the public being at stake, they have a right to demand of the profession a calm, careful and impartial investigation of the claims of homœopathy. It will not do now to turn round and say that homœopathy is all "humbug." The public now know that homœopathy is no humbug; but that it is a matter of fact, and they have a right to insist upon knowing, if allopaths have put homœopathy to the test; and if they have, how and by whom. If they have not, their opinion and denunciation under such circumstances, must be set down as the offspring of presumption or ignorance, and as an attempt to impose their dictum on the credulity of the public, right or wrong.

In order to understand and test homœopathy aright, allopaths would require to devote a very considerable time to the study of it. Rash and unguarded trials only expose the folly and ignorance of their author. Hahnemann was a hard student. The great object he had in view was, the curing of the sick; and to this he devoted all the powers of his great mind. He toiled and laboured for nearly half a century in a way in which he has left few equals; sacrificing ease and comfort, enduring the sneers and persecutions of many enemies. Few of his opponents have ever read his works, and those who have done so, have evidently had only one object in view, namely, to misrepresent and scandalize. The facts recorded in homœopathic writings are different or opposed to those found in allopathic books, therefore they are wrong. This is the way in which many have discussed the subject. They never seem to have thought of the propriety of taking the trouble to prove the truthfulness of the facts by the only method pointed out by the founder of the system. Homœopathy is not like a question in mathematics or metaphysics, which a man may reason out sitting in his arm-chair; it is a simple matter of fact, and as such, must be proved or disproved, as all other facts of the same kind are, namely, by experiment.

What would we think of the man who on reading about the astronomical discoveries of Herschel, should deny the facts, merely because they were entirely different from what he was previously acquainted with; and who should brand the discoverer as a fool and an imposter? and yet this is just the way that homœopathy and its discoverer have been treated, by the great mass of allopaths. We have frequently heard of homœopathy having been tried, and found wanting; but give us the facts connected with the trials, and let us see what they are worth. A man may rub his eyes and eagerly look up to the sky on a fine starry night, and yet entirely fail to verify the facts of the astronomer; but this would not invalidate the facts in the least, certainly not. He must, if he really is in earnest about proving the facts of the astronomer, have a proper telescope, and not only so, but he must learn *how*, and *when* to use it properly. Even so in regard to homœopathy; he must first fully understand the principle, and then he must acquaint himself with the method of putting it in practice properly. No facts of this kind disproving the truth of homœopathy have ever yet been published, while thousands have been published proving its truth. Indeed the evidence in its favour will stand any amount of investigation. Thousands of regularly qualified practitioners have thousands of times in the course of their daily practice, extending over many years, put it to the test of experience, and found it to be true.

It is not possible to conceive of any sufficient object that any of us could have in view in declaring our attachment to homœopathy, unless we had most indubitable evidence of its truth. We are all as well qualified to practice allopathy, as any of our opponents; indeed most of us have done so before we studied homœopathy, and have all the rights and privileges to do so. By doing so, we could greatly benefit ourselves in a worldly point of view; we would have a mighty deal less study; less trouble; less care and anxiety; fewer heartburnings, and slightings from professional brethren; less of the cold shoulder, and less of the evil tongue. But, however painful and unpleasant all these things are, even though they were ten times more we would not flinch from advocating what we believe and *know* to be true. We value truth more than applause, and a good conscience more than many friends. And yet we have great encouragement in our labours. The cause of truth is steadily gaining ground. Thousands who have experienced the healing virtue of homœopathy hail us as benefactors; thousands more are at this moment deriving health and healing from it, even after all other resources had failed, and increasing thousands shall yet taste of its inestimable blessings.

www.ingramcontent.com/pod-product-compliance
Lightning Source LLC
LaVergne TN
LVHW011228110826
845150LV00006B/1576

9781425515027